Designing
Successful
Professional
Meetings
and Conferences
in Education

Designing Successful Professional Meetings and Conferences in Education

Planning,
Implementation,
and Evaluation

Susan Mundry • *Edward Britton*
Senta Raizen • *Susan Loucks-Horsley*

THE NATIONAL INSTITUTE FOR SCIENCE EDUCATION

CORWIN PRESS, INC.
A Sage Publications Company
Thousand Oaks, California

This book is a project of the National Institute for Science Education (NISE), a partnership between the University of Wisconsin-Madison and the National Center for Improving Science Education (NCISE), a division of WestEd. The NISE is supported by the National Science Foundation under Cooperative Agreement No. RED-9452971. Any opinions, findings, and conclusions or recommendations expressed in this publication are those of the authors and do not necessarily reflect the views of the National Science Foundation.

For information:

Corwin Press, Inc.
A Sage Publications Company
2455 Teller Road
CORWIN Thousand Oaks, California 91320
PRESS E-mail: order@corwinpress.com

Sage Publications Ltd.
6 Bonhill Street
London EC2A 4PU
United Kingdom

Sage Publications India Pvt. Ltd.
M-32 Market
Greater Kailash I
New Delhi 110 048 India

Printed in the United States of America

Library of Congress Cataloging-in-Publication Data

Designing successful professional meetings and conferences in education: Planning, implementation, and evaluation / Susan Mundry . . . [et al.]; National Institute for Science Education.
    p. cm.
Includes bibliographical references.
ISBN 0-7619-7632-9 (cloth: alk. paper)
ISBN 0-7619-7633-7 (pbk.: alk. paper)
    1. Forums (Discussion and debate)—Handbooks, manuals, etc. 2. Education—Congresses—Handbooks, manuals, etc. I. Mundry, Susan. II. National Institute for Science Education (U.S.)
LC6519 .D48 2000
370′.68—dc21   00-008537

This book is printed on acid-free paper.

00 01 02 03 04 05 10 9 8 7 6 5 4 3 2 1

Corwin Editorial Assistant: Catherine Kantor
Production Editor: Denise Santoyo
Editorial Assistant: Candice Crosetti
Typesetter/Designer: Marion Warren
Indexer: Kay Dusheck

Contents

Foreword

The authors' idea for a guide to designing and convening effective conferences and meetings has grown over many years of putting together meetings of all sizes, from 6 people to 600 people, convened for various purposes, and from attending many more. In searching for help in their own endeavors, they found some guides that dealt very generally with the what, where, and how of holding conferences, but none that addressed the importance of *designing* meetings to promote learning. This guide emphasizes how to have people work together effectively, understand new ideas, and produce tangible outcomes.

Our perception that such a guide was needed has been reinforced by our experience in conducting Annual Forums for the National Institute for Science Education (NISE). The Forum is the largest and most visible of the Institute's meetings, through which it reaches out to professional organizations, scientific bodies, and educational associations to communicate about its research, help shape its work, and disseminate its findings and recommendations.

The Forum is unusual in that even though it draws 300 individuals from all educational levels and institutions, the various science and mathematics fields, and government and industry, it is designed for a great deal of give-and-take among the participants. It includes opportunities for *ev-*

ery person to contribute to the substance of the discussions, because we learned to design the meeting for productive engagement and learning for all. Similarly, the Forum Proceedings include not only the papers of invited panelists, but also a careful analysis of the discussions and individual think pieces produced by the many other participants. In this way, the Forum is able to draw on the rich expertise of all participants to advance the state of knowledge in a particular area of importance in science and mathematics education.

The authors wrote this guide initially to help all staff and clients of the Institute, but we now hope it will be useful to many more who plan conferences and meetings. We particularly want to thank the National Science Foundation for its continuing support of the Institute and the Annual Forum. Special thanks are due to all our colleagues at the Institute who collaborate with us each year to make the Forum and its proceedings an integral and successful part of our joint endeavor.

Andrew Porter
Director, NISE
Madison, Wisconsin

Preface

The Need for This Guide

Have you ever left a meeting saying to yourself, "What a great meeting—we got so much done and I learned so much"? How about, "What a waste of my time!" or "I can't believe I flew across the country for this. . . . "? Getting these very different reactions is no accident. What meeting designers and facilitators do before, during, and after the meeting will determine the success of the gathering.

This book is intended as a guide for meeting designers and conveners who want to ensure that the meetings they hold are the best they can be. It is premised on the fact that in these turbulent times of constant change, professionals need to make the most of their time and engage in interactions that help them learn and be productive. The book provides guidance, tips, and suggestions for planning professional events that will result in substantial learning for participants. It was written for professionals with all levels of experience in designing meetings and conferences and is based on the authors' experiences with designing and conducting meetings and conferences for people involved in educational reform.

As we attended many meetings, we noticed that certain things worked, while others did not. Many educational events are led by professionals who are teachers or began their careers as teachers. Although they are accomplished at organizing activities for student learning, they may not have considered the different issues involved in organizing meetings and conferences for *adults*. Others may be led by experts who can provide ample information, but may not know how to help the audience apply the new information to their own situation. Since many of the education reform initiatives we work with are focused on science and mathematics education, many of the events we attend are designed by mathematicians and scientists. These meetings tend to be dominated by lectures designed to generate new knowledge and place less emphasis on how one would use the new knowledge. Noticing these design problems and others, we decided to make what we have learned available to others as a guide for planning successful professional meetings.

If you have not designed and run many professional meetings, the value of this guide is obvious. But the guide is also valuable for those who have experience designing and organizing meetings and conferences because it addresses many of the common pitfalls even experienced planners face. Many professionals who do this work often design their meetings intuitively—drawing from the wisdom of past experience and common sense—yet rarely do they document what they did and why, to inform others. This guide makes it a lot easier to mentor staff who are learning how to organize learning events with us.

Further, having a lot of experience in planning events or attending them does not necessarily mean that you have had time or occasion to reflect on what worked and what did not, nor to review resources on effective meeting design. Virtually every time we designed an event in the past, we found we forgot to do something that we already knew was an important design feature or task. We realized we needed to become more purposeful and explicit about why we design meetings the way we do and to document what we learned from our experiences. As one of us likes to say, "Let's make some new mistakes, not repeat ones we've already made!"

Meetings Designed for Learning

Like most professionals, those of us working to promote quality education organize and attend many meetings, work sessions, and conferences each year. The meetings are aimed at spreading new information or knowledge from research and practice, promoting the exchange of new ideas and information, and helping educators learn to implement new practices. There are annual meetings of government agencies, annual and regional meetings sponsored by professional associations, work sessions for project teams to create work products or make project plans, institutes focused on developing new knowledge and skills, and professional development sessions to help educators learn about and apply more effective strategies. As we worked nationally to conduct research on and promote reform in science and mathematics education, we began to ask how these many events could be better organized, more results-oriented, and designed to reflect what we know about adult learning.

We found that it was common for meetings to lack the elements that are essential for making them significant *learning experiences* for participants. For example, participants often come to conferences with little understanding of the outcomes they will derive, and lacking a clear idea of what they will be doing and why. Often, participants do not receive materials ahead of time to prepare them for the meeting. At times the connections between the topic of the meeting and participants' work are not clear enough. Further, some meetings lack mechanisms for maintaining relationships forged during the meeting, such as participant contact information and follow-up communication.

We began to ask, "Are the people who plan these meetings doing all they can to ensure a significant pay-off for the investment they make in planning and convening meetings?" "Is planning and attending such meetings worth the time spent?" "What can be done to improve outcomes?" We decided to encourage people who are working to improve education to use their resources more wisely by producing clearer outcomes and using what is known about adult learning and meeting planning to design and carry out their meetings and conferences.

Experienced conference planners use tried and true methods to make their conferences work. This book is no exception. Its contributors have planned and carried out many educational meetings and attended many, many more. As professional developers in the education field, our mission is to promote more effective use of gatherings, such as conferences, so that they actually produce valuable outcomes. The National Institute for Science Education, a partnership of the University of Wisconsin-Madison and the National Center for Improving Science Education at WestEd, served as a test bed for many of the ideas presented in this book. We took the risk of creating a new kind of conference with the NISE Annual Forum, one that would engage participants in learning from research on science and mathematics while contributing their own knowledge and expertise and connecting NISE's research to their work. We have drawn upon the publication *Designing Professional Development for Teachers of Science and Mathematics* (Loucks-Horsley, Hewson, Love, & Stiles, 1998) as well as other research on effective adult learning and meeting planning to create this guidebook. Additionally, we gathered evaluation information from several mathematics and science reform conferences to determine what did or did not work. We hope we have created a practical, experience-based guide that will: (1) enable you to assess when conferences are the best use of your resources; and (2) help you plan, carry out, and evaluate more effective professional events.

Organization of This Guide

The guide includes five chapters. The first provides background on effective meeting design and management and the principles of adult learning and development—the foundation from which good conferences and meetings are planned. This chapter will help you decide whether holding a meeting is really your best strategy for achieving your desired outcomes. If the answer is yes, Chapters 2 and 3 provide many of the details of planning and organizing meetings and conferences, including what needs to be done when and by whom. Chapter 2 discusses things that must be carefully considered at the outset of designing a meeting: identifying the target audience, setting a budget, selecting a location and date, and assigning responsibilities for further design and planning. Chapter 3 gathers a description and examples of 25 activities that can be used when crafting a detailed agenda. It also provides advice on preparing speakers, sending materials to participants in advance, marketing the conference, and some practical hints for running it. Chapter 4 focuses on the evaluation of the conference, and the final chapter provides guidance on the production of conference proceedings, including a way to systematically capture and analyze participants' discussions during small group sessions. Included throughout the book are checklists, examples, and planning tools.

Acknowledgments

We are grateful to several groups of professionals who made it possible for us over the years to acquire the knowledge for this guide:

- Thousands of professionals who have participated in meetings and conferences that we have organized during our careers, especially those who endured mistakes we made along the way in learning how to create meetings where valuable learning can occur
- Hundreds of professionals who organized meetings and conferences where we were participants and picked up dos and don'ts of effective designing, planning and evaluating
- Every meeting participant who has turned in an evaluation form at one of our events, especially those conscientious people who made time to fill in the open-ended questions

- All of our colleagues at the National Institute for Science Education who were willing to try some innovative designs at the annual NISE Forum

- Susan Millar at the NISE, an evaluator and meeting planner, who collaborated with us especially in designing and planning some effective designs for small-group interactions at the NISE Forum and who produced proceedings documents afterward

- Andy Porter, director of NISE, who always provided critical advice in designing the forum

We also express our sincere appreciation to some people who made it possible to produce this book. Alice Foster, our acquiring editor at Corwin, has given us terrific advice and assistance on this project and all four books that Corwin has recently published from various projects at NCISE/WestEd and NISE. LaDonna Dickerson and Valerie Johnson at NCISE cheerfully endured our edits during the two years it took us to transform our ideas into a complete book. Mary Stenson at WestEd's Learning Innovations provided us with many ideas and tips for this guide. Mary Ann Huntley is a gracious colleague who assisted with editing. We are pleased that the National Science Foundation supported the NISE and its annual NISE Forums. We also thank Larry Suter, our NSF monitor during most of NISE's lifetime, for his active partnership in making the NISE and its Forums a success.

About the Authors and Sponsoring Organizations

Susan Mundry is Senior Research Associate at WestEd where she is a project director for the National Academy of Science and Mathematics Education Leadership and a researcher for the National Institute for Science Education. She is also a partner in ST&C Associates, which helps organizations change and improve through systems thinking. She was formerly the Associate Director of the NETWORK, Inc., a research and development group focused on organizational change and dissemination of innovative educational practice. She is the codeveloper of the "Change Games," two acclaimed simulation boardgames on organizational change called *Making Change for School Improvement and Systems Thinking/Systems Changing.*

Edward Britton is Associate Director of WestEd's National Center for Improving Science Education (NCISE) and is codirector of the NISE team for Interacting with Professional Audiences. He has a lead role in designing, planning and evaluating the annual NISE Forum along with Senta Raizen. He has organized dozens of meetings and conferences within NCISE projects, and previously organized events while serving as project manager for Mary Budd Rowe. He holds a doctoral degree in curriculum and instruction, and bachelor's and master's degrees in chemistry, all from the University of Florida. He began his career teaching sciences at a rural junior-senior high school.

Senta Raizen is Director of the National Center for Improving Science Education and is director of the NISE team for Interacting with Professional Audiences. She has the lead responsibility, along with Edward Britton, for producing the annual NISE Forum. She is lead author or editor of dozens of books and reports produced during a long career that includes leadership roles at NCISE, the National Academy of Sciences, the National Institute for Education, and other prominent organizations. She serves on several national and international advisory boards, including ones for the Third International Mathematics and Science Study (TIMSS) and the National Assessment of Educational Progress (NAEP).

Susan Loucks-Horsley is Director of the Professional Development Team of the NISE and principal investigator of WestEd's National Academy for Science and Mathematics Education Leadership. She also is the associate executive director of the Biological Science Curriculum Study, recently leaving her position as director of Professional Development and Outreach at the NRC's Center for Science, Mathematics, and Engineering Education. She is the lead author of the seminal work *Designing Professional Development for Teachers of Science and Mathematics.* She received her PhD from the University of Texas at Austin, where she helped develop the concerns-based adoption model (CBAM).

The **National Institute for Science Education** (www.nise.org) is a research and development center at the University of Wisconsin-Madison, with a Washington-based partner, the National Center for Improving Science Education. It is directed by Andy Porter and supported by the National Science Foundation through a $10 million, five-year collaborative agreement. The Institute has several teams, including one for Professional Development and another for Interacting with Professional Audiences, which is responsible for the annual NISE Forum.

The **National Center for Improving Science Education,** a division of WestEd (www.wested.org/ncise), is a partner in the NISE. The NCISE is known for leading the field in professional development, evaluation, curriculum analysis and assessment approaches. Consistent with its mission to bridge the gaps between research and practice, the NCISE role within NISE is to help disseminate NISE research through the annual Forum and other activities.

CORWIN
PRESS

The Corwin Press logo—a raven striding across an open book—represents the happy union of courage and learning. We are a professional-level publisher of books and journals for K-12 educators, and we are committed to creating and providing resources that embody these qualities. Corwin's motto is "Success for All Learners."

1

The Knowledge Base of Effective Meetings and Conferences

This chapter will help you decide whether to hold a meeting or consider some other way to meet your objectives. It then reviews the knowledge of effective meetings and adult learning.

Conferences Should Be the Best They Can Be

Well-done conferences or meetings require a major investment of time and other resources. They are extremely expensive in both costs to conveners and the time and travel costs to participants. They have to be very good for their benefits to outweigh their costs. Consider this: a 2-day event involving 200 people costs the audience about $400,000 in labor and travel expenses—for every hour of time the cost is $25,000! Is your activity and your design for it worth that audience investment? Do you consciously keep the participants' valuable time and considerable expense in mind and honor that by ensuring they will get the greatest possible return for their investment?

When you fully consider how expensive meetings are, you realize the high stakes of holding them. To make them worthwhile, they must be good. Good meetings and conferences produce clearly defined outcomes.

They are often about promoting new learning, connected to participants' own situations. Good meetings bring people together in respectful ways to do work they couldn't do alone.

As you plan your next meeting, we challenge you to hold yourself to a set of principles that will lead you to go beyond business as usual to produce an event that yields more valuable outcomes.

Nine Principles Held by Effective Meeting Designers

1. Establish and share clear outcomes

2. Design activities to engage all participants

3. Model effective learning processes and environments (In science and mathematics education particularly, we found meetings to be an opportunity to model effective teaching and learning strategies. For example, at a recent conference of the National Institute for Science Education, a participant observed that the meeting was designed with as much time to process information as to generate it. She remarked how that feature had given her the time to reflect on what she heard and think about what it meant for her own situation. Although there are no absolute formulas for the perfect meeting design, all should strive to model what we know about adult learning and engagement.)

4. Establish clear roles

5. Have participants take responsibility for reaching the stated outcomes

6. Connect with participants' own work and thinking

7. Provide opportunities for continued learning and maintaining relationships after the event

8. Encourage participants to share what they learned with others outside the meeting

9. Provide ample time for reflecting on the information and experiences

Your commitment to these principles will help you create meetings that promote change or growth, reach clear outcomes, and help people develop new relationships. With the scarce resources available for mathematics and science education, if you can't do a good conference, don't do one at all. If you decide you want to do one, plan an effective meeting that reflects the principles and knowledge outlined in this section.

Why Have a Conference or Meeting—
Is This the Best Strategy for Meeting Your Goals?

People have many demands on their time. They must make choices about how to spend it. Before you decide to have a conference or meeting, consider what you want to accomplish. Are you trying to create a community around your work? Is your aim to establish an agenda for future work for research or a development effort? Are you trying to solve a particular problem for which certain expertise is needed? Do you want to get multiple perspectives on an issue?

Holding conferences is a good strategy when you want to establish an annual or regular time for people to come together to be a part of your work or organization or to get updates that help them stay connected to your work. Many conferences are annual events like this that enable people to have a continuing experience with your organization and its work. The National Institute for Science Education (NISE) instituted an Annual Forum for this purpose. The event created a regular time each year for education stakeholders to learn from the work of the NISE and apply new knowledge and approaches to the improvement of science and mathematics education. Professional associations hold similar national and regional meetings, bringing together members to network and share new information. For this type of meeting it is critical to build in ways for participants to stay connected to you (and to each other, as necessary) throughout the year or from event to event. For example, use e-mail, list serves, newsletters, regional group meetings, and other strategies to maintain relationships and keep connected to stakeholder groups for networking. Are you trying to create a group of people to follow and perhaps disseminate your work or to become members of your group or association? If so, creating a regular time for them to come together to update their knowledge or skills and renew relationships would be an effective strategy for you.

Conferences are also a good idea when the goal is making decisions or solving problems, e.g., the participants review and weigh evidence and information, generate ideas, make decisions or recommendations, or solve problems. In this type of meeting, it is important for participants to hear one another's point of view and come to consensus. For example, as state education agencies and local school districts make decisions about how to reform their education systems, it is important for members of these groups to have opportunities to create a common vision of what the new program will look like in action. As new strategies and practices are tried out, follow-up conferences can be held to share successes, learn from mistakes, and generate ideas for solving common problems. A conference works well for this type of work as long as it is facilitated, ensuring that the people you bring together communicate directly and share ideas, information and perspectives.

Are you working with a group of people who are beginning an organizational change effort or confronting problems as they implement new practices? Do they have experience that they can contribute to help solve problems? Have you provided them with information or facilitated the collection of materials and information that will drive a productive problem-solving session? If so, an event that helps them make decisions and/or address problems makes sense.

Another important purpose for a conference is to disseminate new ideas, products, and/or results from recent work—ultimately to promote use of these in some way. The educational reform movement has used national and regional conferences as a strategy to disseminate and build commitment to the national and state-level visions for reform with wide audiences and to receive feedback on ideas. Developers of new products and researchers use this strategy to build interest in using their products and applying their research findings. For example, do you have new research information that is important to a particular target group such as teachers or school administrators, and are you interested in engaging with these audiences about how they might use these new materials or findings? If so, then it is appropriate to bring them together to learn about the new findings and to discuss what they can contribute to educational practice. What do the findings mean? How big of a change do they constitute in practice? What would practitioners need to do to make them a reality in the classroom? These types of meetings provide a forum in which practitioners can test new ideas and give researchers and developers the grounding they need to refine new ideas and products. Regional meetings held to disseminate the National Science Education Standards (NSES) are a good example of this type of meeting. During these sessions, educators learned about the NSES and worked with them to discover how they could infuse the standards into their work. The research on effective dissemination cautions, however, that the events must be followed by other communication and "sustained interactions" to promote the actual use of new ideas and practices (Hutchinson & Huberman, 1993).

When your goal is to conduct more one-way dissemination, i.e., get products and ideas that have already been tested and refined out to people without receiving their feedback or providing them with assistance to learn or use the product, conferences are not usually the most cost effective strategy. Other strategies such as print and electronic communication are more cost effective in these cases. When your goal is to get feedback, promote learning, or plan actions around results of your work, it makes sense to bring people together because you often learn more from the participants' interactions than you learn from what they say individually.

Another good reason for holding a conference or meeting is to create awareness of a need and to inspire participants to take action to address it. This type of conference is often aimed at bringing together diverse stakeholders of particular issues and motivating them to become advocates for addressing a shared problem. Often these meetings will also establish networks of like-minded individuals working toward similar goals. For example, conferences are an effective strategy for setting a reform agenda. Participants who have some stake in the reform come together to assess needs, craft the case for change, generate models and ideas, and discuss how to engage others.

Finally, all events aimed at improving education should promote learning new concepts and ideas, which is enhanced by interaction with other learners and sharing of perspectives. Such conferences should *model* effective teaching and learning processes and show participants new ways to engage learners, thereby encouraging them to take back the process, as well as the content, to their own settings. These meetings should always build in opportunities for follow-up contact.

As you consider the question "Why have a conference?" think about your purposes in convening a conference. Are there other means that achieve the same results? Would print, electronic, or teleconference communication be a better way for you to achieve your goals? If you believe in-person interaction is *essential* to your goals, what will you do to ensure that there is a substantial pay-off for participants?

In the education business, meetings are often planned and held as part of many projects because "we've always done it that way." Sometimes the meeting's only real purpose is to check off a tangible milestone in a project plan or proposal. We need to rethink this practice. Educators are working to reduce wasted time in classrooms and ensure learning for all. So, too, education reformers must guarantee that their activities are designed to produce significant results. The next subsections summarize the key knowledge conference planners should draw upon to design effective learning opportunities.

Characteristics of Effective Meetings and Conferences

Like any other effective practice, conferences and meetings designed to achieve their objectives have a set of characteristics that contribute to their success (Friel & Bright, 1997; Loucks-Horsley, Hewson, Love, & Stiles, 1998; Nadler & Nadler, 1987; Scholtes, Joiner, & Streibel, 1996). When these characteristics are present, the event has a greater likelihood of achieving its purposes and desired outcomes. These include:

- *Clear Purpose and Outcomes.* Expectations for conveners and participants are clear and stated in conversations, e-mail, agenda, written invitations, brochures, or registration forms. What are your expectations for the participants? What are your purposes and how will you communicate them to the participants? What will the participants gain from your event?
- *Organization and Logistics.* Logistics, such as location, time, transportation, materials, and food, are often seen as the minor details of the event. But they can make or break the day. How will you ensure smooth operations and address the "creature comfort needs" of your participants? If your participants are uncomfortable with the room temperature, the amount or quality of food, etc., it makes it harder for them to concentrate on the agenda. If you make plans to meet their needs but fail to communicate these plans to them, you will also lose their attention as participants wonder where and when they can eat lunch or if there is time to go to the restroom. Put yourself in the participants' shoes! Too often, meetings fail to respect these legitimate needs and only address them as an afterthought.
- *Value.* People who attend the event are investing in learning something new, getting ideas, help, or benefiting in some way. Meeting planners often focus on accomplishing *their* goal and do not think about what is in it for the participants. What value are you offering to people who attend your event? Why should they choose your meeting over something else?
- *Variety.* Daylong and multi-day events must be interspersed with a variety of interactions. Mixing up the types of learning activities and the groupings of people as much as possible is essential for addressing different needs and styles and for maintaining attention span. Are you planning a variety of experiences for your participants? At the same time, don't address this superficially—throwing in a variety of activities for the sake of variety. Each varied activity must make sense, articulate well with the preceding and following activities, and address your purpose. The overall set of program elements should have a logical and feasible flow.
- *Networking.* In evaluations of conferences and meetings, people consistently rate the opportunity to meet and talk with interesting and knowledgeable people as one of the main benefits of conference attendance. What mechanisms have you created to encourage networking? Event organizers may incorrectly think that participants will connect with other people after hours. The chances are high

that if you don't sanction networking as a legitimate conference outcome and build in opportunities for networking, participants will skip some of your program activities to accomplish this aim. The NISE Forums provided lunches to keep participants together and allotted 90 minutes to give ample time to talk as well as eat, and announced this aim to the participants.

- *Effective Use of Time.* Think carefully about the use of your meeting time. It should be used and managed to make every minute count. Use only those activities that are interactive and require communication and discussion. To the extent possible, activities that can be done outside of the meeting such as reading, thinking about and responding to questions, and so on should be done prior to the meeting. Have an activity or questions posted on an overhead projector or chart paper for early arrivals to serve as a conversation starter that gets them meeting and talking with others as soon as they arrive. Breaks can be structured to encourage networking. How will you make the best use of everyone's time?
- *Quality of Leaders and Facilitators.* There are multiple roles that must be played in an effective meeting. Presenters and leaders must have demonstrated knowledge and skills as speakers, facilitators, and problem-solvers. They must know their subject thoroughly and be flexible enough to make adjustments to their audience or working group. What standards do you have for the leaders and facilitators you choose for your event? How do you communicate expectations and assess the fit between what you need and what the leader can offer?
- *Ongoing Evaluation.* Effective meetings and conferences are assessed before, during, and after the event. Data are gathered and used to make improvements and to build on successes. Get better advance "buy-in" and improved activities by circulating a draft agenda for participant reaction and by doing your best to address their feedback. For a larger event, formally or informally create a design team that includes key staff from the sponsors. But, be sure to include people who represent key target audiences. What methods do you use for gathering and analyzing evaluation information? How do you use this information to make changes in your work?
- *Quality of Content and Design.* The content presented in conferences and meetings needs to reflect credible, sound, current, and interesting knowledge. The meeting design should make use of the best structures and formats for engaging and enlightening participants. To ensure success, it is essential that meeting planners know the content and designs leaders will use and provide feedback and suggestions to adjust the program to the targeted audience. It is essential for planners to help presenters know the audience they will

have and what the audience expects. If possible, attend a session led by the presenters ahead of time or request that they send you a videotape. Work with them to be sure they understand your goals and that the design will address these goals adequately. Decide whom you want and figure out the best way to get them. Sometimes it takes finding the right person to sign the letter of invitation. Sometimes listing a recognized association as a cosponsor adds to your recruitment success. How do you communicate with meeting leaders about what they have planned? Do you encourage leaders to provide references and examples as evidence of their claims? How do you find out and communicate participants' expectations? What do you know about the presenter's style and how it will work with your participants?

- *Resources*. It is impossible to cover everything about a topic in the limited time available for most meetings. Providing resource lists, displays, poster sessions, and exhibits can help people access additional information about the subject of your conference or meeting. What mechanism do you include in your meetings to inform participants of other available resources?
- *Products*. It is rewarding for participants to come away from a meeting with a tangible product that they contributed to during the meeting. Plans, models, or new ideas can all be productive outputs from meetings. After meetings, summary documents or conference proceedings that capture the interactions and learning from the event should be prepared. What tangible products could result from your meeting?
- *Right Audience*. Having the right mix of people who are knowledgeable and interested in the meeting topics is essential. Meeting planners need to know who would benefit most from the meeting and target participation accordingly. Although diverse audiences are often desirable, there is a challenge in designing the meeting to be relevant for all participants. Who is your target audience? How are you going to get them to your event? How can you tailor the meeting design and content to encourage optimal participation?

Pay Attention to Design

Like effective professional development, good meetings and conferences are designed to address specific inputs. A model for thinking about design is represented in Figure 1.1. This model suggests that planning and imple-

Figure 1.1. Professional Development Design Process for Mathematics and Science Education Reform

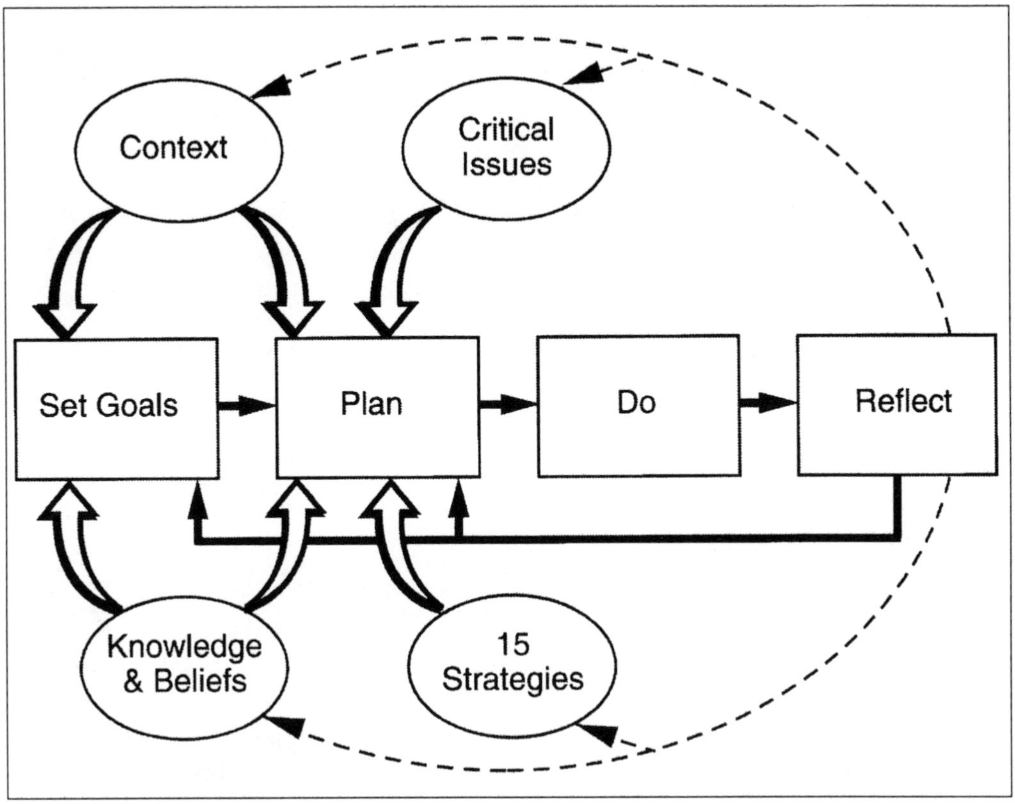

SOURCE: Loucks-Horsley et al., 1998.

menting professional learning opportunities is enhanced when designers address a number of elements, including clarifying goals and purposes, identifying knowledge and beliefs, and assessing the context in which you are working. Since many conferences and meetings are tied to more ongoing professional development, successful designers must establish the role that their conferences play in the larger initiative. They plan for the design to change over time to keep pace with changes in the environment. In addition, they know that people's needs, skills, and knowledge change over time as they engage in learning, requiring that the professional development program or plan shift to stay aligned with needs (Mundry & Loucks-Horsley, 1999). For more information on the design framework, see *Designing Professional Development for Teachers of Science and Mathematics* (Loucks-Horsley et al., 1998).

Principles of Effective Adult Learning

One of the knowledge bases planners must understand and use is on adult learning. Designers need to know how adults learn and the characteristics of effective professional development. In summarizing research on professional learning experiences in education—many of which are conducted within conferences and meetings—Loucks-Horsley et al. (1998) suggest that adult learners develop new knowledge by constructing it for themselves. They say "the construction of knowledge is a process of change that includes addition, creation, modification, refinement, restructuring, and rejection" (p. 36).

Studies of adult development have indicated several conditions necessary for adult learning. These include:

- Opportunity to try out new ideas and practices
- Careful and continuous guided reflection and discussion about the proposed ideas or changes
- Continuity of program and time for significant change
- Personal support, as well as challenge, during the process of changing ideas or practices (Sprinthall & Sprinthall, 1983)

Creating events that provide opportunities for people to learn means creating environments in which they can look at what they know through different lenses and try on new ideas. Adult learners need opportunities to safely explore questions about how something they already know connects to new concepts and ideas and to examine and modify their thinking as they challenge assumptions and beliefs. As Fosnot states (quoted in Brooks & Brooks (1993), "Learning is not discovering more but interpreting through a different scheme or structure."

Conferences whose purpose is learning often rely on strategies that enable participants to recall or apply knowledge. We must think beyond this when the goal is to engage people around new ideas that often do not fit with people's current thinking. When this happens the learners experience a "disconnect" or dissonance between what they have known and what they are now encountering. Such "cognitive dissonance" creates tension as they struggle to make sense. These moments create real opportunities for break-through thinking (Thompson & Zeuli, 2000). Creating environments that promote such engagement is challenging. It requires that we understand, articulate, and begin to challenge assumptions we hold, and the lenses through which we make meaning and learn (Senge, 1990; Senge, Keiner, Roberts, Ross, & Smith, 1994). It requires time to explore and to test out new ideas, as well as offering guidance and support to refine new knowledge. Meetings that reach these standards are becoming the norm in organizations that have a professional culture for learning. In these places, "learning communities" are developing. Meetings are characterized by dialogues in which people suspend their assumptions and work with colleagues, often using data to understand the underlying problems or complex ideas.

Ultimately, making the most of conferences and meetings as learning opportunities requires that meeting planners help participants make meaning of the event for themselves (Ramsborg, 1995). Conference planning is, therefore, an art. It requires: knowledge of the audience; meticulous attention to logistical details; varied pacing; opportunities for participants to actively engage with information; stimulating facilitators, presenters, or teachers; availability of print and electronic resources; an environment conducive to learning; ongoing monitoring; and follow-up.

Conferences held for people in the science and mathematics education reform movement require planners to address the special challenges associated with this work. Where are the participants in the process? Are they just beginning and need to understand what effective science and mathematics education looks like? Or are they further along in the change process, when they need time to reflect on what they have done, or meet with a "critical friend" who can help them begin to assess impact and decide what is the next step? Do you have the resources and flexibility to accommodate such diversity with one meeting or conference, or would smaller multiple meetings be more effective? Whatever the primary purpose of your meeting may be (informing the audience about research in curriculum and instruction, showcasing new programs, or creating debate about cutting-edge issues), it must incorporate principles that guide learning (e.g., inquiry, reflection, and content knowledge); and it must address the level of knowledge and skills of the participants.

2

Early Planning

In Chapter 1, you considered the purposes of your meeting and the knowledge of effective practices for designing a conference or meeting. This chapter and Chapter 3 will help you design your meeting, addressing the many details necessary to ensure that your events are the best they can be. Although these chapters discuss design issues in detail, they do not always get into the nuts and bolts of how to execute a conference. For such detailed assistance, consult a professional meeting planner manual such as the 700+ pages of *Professional Meeting Management, 3rd Edition* by E.G. Polivka (1996). Resource A illustrates the range of topics that can be found in such manuals.

Identify the Target Audience

Having the right people at your meeting is essential. Whom are you targeting for participation? Whose perspectives are essential to your goals and outcomes? What can you do to ensure equity of participation in the meeting?

Identify the people who are closest to and have the influence to take action on the issue or focus of your meeting or conference. For example, if your goal is to establish a consensus about education reform within a state, you must identify the many different people who have a stake in education in your state. These could include staff from statewide projects, parents, teachers, business leaders, faculty from colleges and universities, scientists, state education agency staff, and professional developers, to name just a few.

Conference planners too often invite only the people they know. When considering your audience for a meeting or conference you need to "cast a wide net." As you identify participants for your meeting, be sure and include a diverse representation by gender, race, ethnicity, role, and perspective. Sometimes when trying to reach quite varied audiences (e.g., teachers, the research community, the technical assistance providers, policymakers, etc.), you will need to plan different conferences or carefully craft an agenda that involves all of these audiences interacting together around issues that are of mutual interest. Unfortunately, some audiences are not accustomed to working together. Therefore, it takes a skilled planner to create an agenda that meets multiple needs and/or includes multiple audiences. However, because we need to build wide consensus on reform, it is increasingly important to create venues in which these varied audiences can work together.

As you think about your audience and what they might gain from your meeting or conference, maintain a bias toward impact. By this, we suggest that you identify the results you desire from the conference and hold yourself accountable for attaining these results. What does this have to do with targeting your audience? Often conference designers anticipate results that are not within the power or purview of the participants. If the goal of a conference is to develop plans for updating curriculum, the decision-makers related to this issue must be present or somehow involved in supporting the effort. Otherwise the participants may be thwarted in achieving the results the conference planners envision.

Think about the participants you are targeting for your meeting. Who are they? What do they want to gain from the meeting? What and who do they influence? What are their interests or objectives? How can you address their varied needs and interests effectively?

Conference Budget

We mentioned in the first chapter that you should establish a budget to consider the cost and benefit of holding a meeting in the first place. So, creating a budget for your meeting is one of the first activities that should be done.

As soon as you begin to plan your meeting, think about *all* the costs you will incur and plan for how you will meet them. Many conferences charge a registration fee to either cover the costs entirely or to defray costs that cannot be covered by a project grant or institutional funds. Your budget should be an important consideration when making decisions about site, numbers of staff and presenters, date for the event and promotional plans. As you plan your meeting budget, allocate funds for the following: presenter/leader fees, travel, facilities, meals, supplies, staff time, advertising, mailing, equipment, reproduction of conference materials, and follow-up mailings (e.g., a conference proceedings). If you plan to charge participants for their participation, generate a budget of all of your possible costs and divide them by the number of participants anticipated. This will give you an idea if you can cover your costs. Depending on the type of conference, participants may expect to pay anywhere from $15-25 to defray the cost of their materials or lunch and up to $500-2000 for multi-day training sessions. Other possible revenues that you might generate to cover your costs include sales of tapes or conference proceedings, exhibitor fees, and contributions from cosponsors. In-kind contributions of time, supplies, and resources can also be solicited from participants, leaders, and sponsors.

Think about strategies that will help you control expenditures. Holding meetings over weekends enables conference leaders and participants to get reduced airfares. Having cosponsors may provide speakers at no cost to the conference. Using your own facility or donated space reduces the cost of hotel facilities and food expenses. Also check your assumptions about costs. For example, it is sometimes less expensive to send out conference notebooks to be copied and collated than to do it in-house, if you consider the cost of your staff labor in addition to materials and copying charges. Figure 2.1 is a budget worksheet. Use this to generate your budget very early in the planning process.

One of the most commonly and severely underestimated conference costs is the staff time needed to design, execute, and follow up a conference! Later in this chapter, we'll discuss being clear about who is doing what. Before making those decisions, however, you have to have a detailed, comprehensive list of what needs to be done. How often have you sat exhausted even *before* your conference or meeting, knowing that an awful lot of your time has been consumed not only in getting ready, but being unable to pin down just what the time was spent on? The problem is, you probably did not sufficiently detail the tasks before you started.

Figure 2.1. Budget Worksheet

Expenses:

Meeting Planning, Design, and Execution

   Staff/Consultants   _____

   Fee/Salary   _____

   Other Expenses

               Total Planning/Design Expenses _____

Marketing

   Brochures, Design, and
   Printing   _____

   Advertising   _____

   Mailing Lists   _____

   Postage   _____

               Total Marketing _____

Office Supplies and Expenses

   Stationery
   (Notebooks/Folders/Name
   Badges)   _____

   Telephone, Fax   _____

   Postage, Shipping   _____

               Total Office Supplies _____

Prepaid Expenses

   Deposits   _____

   Insurance   _____

               Total Prepaid Expenses _____

Other Expenses

   Agenda Book/Conference
   Folder   _____

   Audiovisual Equipment   _____

   Awards and Mementos   _____

   Computer Services   _____

   Exhibit Spaces   _____

   Field Trips   _____

   Follow-up   _____

   Gratuities   _____

   Ground Transportation   _____

   Hospitality Suite   _____

Figure 2.1. Continued

Interpreters, Translators	_____	
Participant packets	_____	
Printing and Reproduction	_____	
Public Relations	_____	
Shipping	_____	
Signs	_____	
	Total Other Expenses	_____
Presenters/Facilitators		
Accommodations	_____	
Travel	_____	
Honoraria and Fees	_____	
	Total Presenters/ Facilitator Expenses	_____
Site		
Sleeping Rooms	_____	
Meeting Rooms	_____	
Food and Beverage	_____	
	Total Site Expenses	_____
Total Expenses		_____
Income		
Registration Fees	_____	
Grants/Project Budget	_____	
Exhibitors	_____	
Co-Sponsors	_____	
Other	_____	
Total Income		_____
Gross Income		_____
Less:		_____
	Total Expenses	_____
	Income after expenses	_____
	NET Profit (Loss)	_____

Some things that sound quick can actually be laborious. For example, "inviting" people can involve many tasks: identifying the kinds of participants involved; compiling contact information; arranging to buy mailing lists; determining whether electronic lists are compatible with your in-house database; writing the invitation letter; arranging for its production; and acquiring needed supplies and assembling the mailing. Perhaps nothing specific in the above list surprised you, but if you don't make a list that fits your situation, you could be shocked when your time greatly exceeds your estimate. So, *carefully* consider the time and therefore the cost of detailed tasks hidden behind each of the major design activities, such as working with speakers and making site arrangements.

Identify Cosponsors or Partners

If you are planning a large conference and wish to draw upon the constituencies of key organizations or send a message about a strategic alliance, you may want to recruit a limited number of cosponsors. Cosponsors bring credibility and sometimes financial support; however, they also have expectations about what they will get out of their investment and may want to exert some control over the content and/or the presenters for your event. It is also important for you to explore how the cosponsoring organization is viewed by your target audience to be sure that they are an asset to you and to negotiate clear expectations about their involvement and control. Any exploration with cosponsors should be discussed with leaders in your own organization to ensure that the cosponsor is a good fit with your organization's beliefs, philosophy, and approach.

Finding cosponsors is often like deciding which relatives to invite to the wedding; it snowballs and you find that once you ask one, you have to ask ten more. Having a few cosponsors can be beneficial, but too many can be a huge distraction. Weigh carefully what cosponsors will contribute and limit your numbers to those that are most strategic for you.

Select Location and Date

Call key people you must have at your conference before setting a date. Be sure to check to see that dates do not conflict with other professional meetings, particularly during the period of January through April when many professional associations in education hold their annual meetings. Investigate sites for your meeting to find out the type of facilities available, accessibility to technology displays, ease of getting participants to the site, cost, and dates available. Make sure that your site is handicapped accessible and that hotel rooms are available for out-of-town participants.

If you have a lot of flexibility about your location, look into cities with special airfare deals, select places that are easy to get to, places where you have secretarial support available, or places that offer special attractions. If you choose a "destination spot" for your conference, be sure to allow down time for people to see the attractions or you may lose them during the scheduled meeting. For example, start early in the morning, break early in the afternoon, and reconvene for an evening session. This gives participants time during the day to enjoy their surroundings without missing important parts of the meeting. Call conference planners in your professional associations and ask them about different facilities in different cities. They have often visited the facilities and can provide an unbiased view of whether a site would meet your needs. If possible, visit the sites yourself to see how they will work for you. A city's convention bureau can be a great resource in providing site information and even arranging a site visit for you. We have had bureaus pay for our travel expenses when the event was for 200+ people. Use the "Site Selection Checklist" in Figure 2.2 to ensure that the site meets your needs.

Figure 2.2. Site Selection Worksheet

Location
_____ How much crime has recently been experienced in the area?
_____ What parking is available and what is the cost for local attendees?
_____ Does the city have a convention bureau that will help identify sites?
_____ How accessible is the site for all participants?
_____ Is the site convenient to public transportation? To airports?
_____ What is the climate of the site at the time the conference will be held?
_____ What is the distance between the various hotels and the meeting site?
_____ What are the aesthetics of the site and its surroundings?
_____ What off-site excursions, entertainment, and restaurants would be accessible?

Past History
_____ Have you or others you know used this site before and been satisfied?
_____ Have you requested and checked site references?

Service Facilities
_____ What recreational/health facilities are provided onsite or nearby?
_____ Does the site charge any fees for using the facilities?
_____ Are there on-site business services, such as fax, copying, and modem phone lines?

(continued)

Figure 2.2. Continued

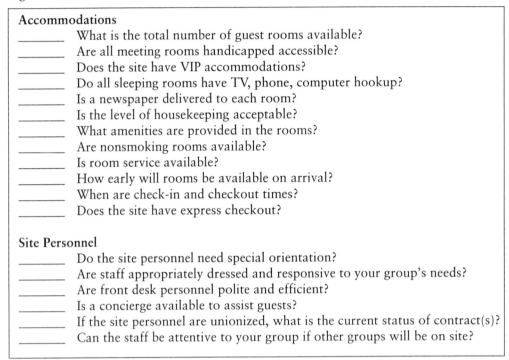

You never know which item in Figure 2.2 might negatively affect your event if you forget to consider it. To illustrate our point (and for your amusement), here are two stories that have happened to us. For a recent NISE Forum, we neglected to ask what other groups were scheduled to be in the hotel during our event. As a result, some Forum participants were tired at the opening session because of an incident the night before. It turns out that an organization in the beverage industry was ending their conference the day before ours. In the middle of the night, several of their participants got rowdy and pulled the hotel's fire alarms, forcing the evacuation of some of our participants! A second example comes from several years ago. We neglected to ask the hotel whether any renovations were scheduled for the time of our event. Participants ended up having to walk through awkward and ugly construction scaffolding to arrive at our event instead of the beautiful lobby we saw when the contract was signed. Some participants could not concentrate on small group discussions because workers were hammering away.

Assign Responsibility for Conference Design and Planning

Once you have decided to plan a conference, designate one person as the coordinator of the event. There also should be one person designated to handle all logistical plans, although these two functions—coordination of planning and design and logistical arrangements—must be tightly coupled since the decisions made for one affect the other.

For large conferences, planners often appoint a design committee and assign responsibility for different parts of the conference to committee members. The people responsible for the conference should meet regularly to review plans and milestones and update one another on progress. Between meetings, use e-mail to send updates on developments to everyone concerned. Figure 2.3, Sample Agenda for Team Meetings, and Figure 2.4, Conference/Meeting Planning and Responsibilities Chart, will help you with your planning.

Figure 2.3. Sample Agenda for Team Meetings

Instructions: This is a sample agenda for your planning meetings. The items marked with an asterisk should be included in the team's first meeting and revisited as necessary.

Project _____ Meeting
Date_____

1. Review agenda (5 mins.)

   Explain the goals of this meeting. Review the time needed for each item. Note which items must be completed today.

2.* Brief self-introductions by team members (10 mins.)

   Even when team members know one another, it is a good idea to allow time for everyone to share something about their current work and how it relates to the team's purpose.

3. Review the purpose of the team (15 mins.)

   State the purpose of the team and remind members of what needs to be accomplished.

4.* Discuss the roles of team leader, coach or advisor, and team members (15 mins.)

5.* Set ground rules (15 mins.)
   Generate group ground rules such as beginning and ending on time, respecting one another's opinions, expecting full participation, etc.

(continued)

Figure 2.3. Continued

6.* Introduce basic concepts or skills needed for the work (15 mins.)

  If you are beginning your meeting planning, refer especially to the Planning and Responsibilities Chart in Figure 2.4.

7. Discuss assignments for the next meeting: date, time (10 mins.)

  Identify the activities that team members should undertake before the next meeting.

8. Meeting evaluation (10 mins.)

  Assess whether the meeting objectives were met and ground rules were followed; and, the participation level of the members. Ask for ideas for improving the next meeting.

Figure 2.4. Conference/Meeting Planning and Responsibilities Chart

Title of Conference/Meeting_____

Date_____   Place_____

Conference Coordinator/Manager_____

Activity	Person Responsible	Tasks	Status (as of date)	Check Off
Conference Committee				
Site Selection				
Marketing				
Budget				
Speakers and Session Leaders				
Staff and Resource People				
Exhibitions				

(continued)

Figure 2.4. Continued

Activity	Person Responsible	Tasks	Status (as of date)	Check Off
Registration				
Meeting Room Logistics and Food				
Audiovisual and Technology				
Public Relations				
Participant Notebooks & Handouts				
Evaluation				
Conference Proceedings				
Travel Arrangements				
Contracts With Speakers and Leaders				

3

Detailed Design Issues

While Chapter 2 discussed critical planning that must be done at the outset of deciding to hold a meeting or conference, Chapter 3 describes vital decisions in planning and executing the detailed agenda for educational events. A majority of the chapter describes a portfolio of 25 activities that you can consider when putting together a program. The balance of the chapter discusses supporting speakers and facilitators, marketing the conference, providing advance materials to participants, and some practical hints for running the conference.

Decide on Activities and Approaches

For many conferences, planners invite experts, leading thinkers, facilitators, scientists, and researchers to make presentations in a large group format. Although this format can be useful for spreading new information or inspiring action, it alone will not produce the kind of changes in thinking and action that we are often seeking. When you do use presentations such as these, it is essential for you to think carefully about how your presenters will engage the audience in new thinking and ideas.

Conference and meeting designers should avoid overuse of lectures. Instead, they need to *vary* activities and provide ample opportunities for participants to work with and understand new information and concepts presented. Participants need time to apply it to their own purposes. Drawing on the knowledge summarized in Chapter 1, the designer needs to ensure that the environment supports a productive meeting.

Ingredients for Success

- Activities are interactive and engage participants
- Purpose and outcomes are clear
- Agenda and presentations are organized to meet the purposes
- Meeting is well-facilitated
- There are clear next steps

For example, a NSF-supported conference on kindergarten through sixth grade mathematics education in North Carolina was designed for the purpose of exploring the following central question: What do we know about professional development in mathematics that can inform the design of large-scale teacher enhancement programs for optimal impact? The conference involved many experts who had designed and implemented programs to enhance teaching. Commonly, this type of meeting would have been designed to give the experts a set amount of time on the agenda to present the background, features, and findings of their programs. However, the organizers of this meeting wanted to ensure that all participants had the opportunity to really *engage* with the information presented and to think how it would translate into each of their particular circumstances. Therefore, they created an interactive forum where participants conversed with leading science and mathematics professionals around issues of reform and how the issues related to the participants' work.

The conference organizers also identified a clear and explicit focus on several different areas of information they hoped to generate at the conference (e.g., identifying the generic principles to guide development of teacher enhancement programs and alternative strategies and options for current teacher enhancement programs) (Friel & Bright, 1997). To accomplish this, organizers developed four issues papers to inform participants and to help them reflect on the meeting purpose. These were distributed so participants could read them before the meeting. At the conference, the authors of the issues papers presented short sessions with the goal of looking for contradictions, in a sense "hunting for the truth." As a next step, working groups were formed to relate the issues and the participants' experiences and to make recommendations related to the topics of the conference. As a result, the participants developed one-page descriptions of how their projects related to the purpose and issues of the meeting.

There are many types of approaches and activities that can be considered as you design your conference. Highly interactive working sessions such as the one described above can be very productive and rewarding. Other conferences need to provide many different kinds of experiences simultaneously for a diverse audience. For large conferences, convene a design committee to set the agenda for your conference. The design committee can be comprised of project staff, staff from a cosponsoring organization, and a representative of the conference audience. For smaller meetings, project staff serve as the design committee. The design committee is responsible for brainstorming ideas for facilitators, speakers, and topics for the meeting and developing the draft agenda. The committee should identify possible presenters and a range of formats (e.g., panel discussions that are pre-arranged and planned with built-in time for audience response, interactive workshops, lectures, and small group activities). If the conference is being held over several days, the committee should also plan evening activities and speakers. Alternatively, if participants need some time off, have suggestions available for food and entertainment.

The committee should create a list of expectations about the topics, what participants will learn and the format for each session (e.g., interactive, based on principles of adult learning, addressing multiple learning styles). Review these verbally and in writing with the leaders or presenters for the meeting.

Create scenarios of how the day may unfold; e.g., map out plenary sessions, small group meetings, role-alike group discussions, action planning sessions, and on-going display areas. Anticipate how people will flow through the different sessions to spot potential problems. Meeting designs that only expect participants to "sit and git"—sit in their seats and listen to others make presentations throughout the meeting—are unacceptable. Activities should be planned to encourage movement, participation, and deep learning. Plan to provide opportunities for participants to reflect on each session, either during the last 15 minutes of a session, or an end-of-the-day wrap-up session. Build in 15-20 minute breaks—conference participants repeatedly say the opportunity to meet and talk to new colleagues is as important as attending sessions. See Resource B for sample agendas.

As you design your activities, think about how people will select or move to activities such as small-group or break-out sessions. Ask people for their choices during sign-up and on the registration form. Assign people to rooms and teams ahead of time and identify facilitators for small groups. Depending on the meeting, you may assign people purposively or randomly. Either way, organize lists or code nametags with room numbers so that people know where to go.

Keep your purpose in mind as you design the meeting. Select activities that are designed to reach your purpose. In general, we recommend that every meeting or conference that has learning as a goal include the following elements (Bybee, 1997). Create a design for your meeting that

---

Elements of the Design

1. Introduction Activity: Participants learn the outcomes, generate ground rules, and review the agenda.
2. Engagement Activity: Participants engage in an ice-breaker that gives them a chance to think about what they know and their past experiences and connect these to what they will do in the meeting.
3. Exploring Knowledge and Ideas: Participants learn while doing, by exploring new ideas through discussion, simulation, case study, or hands-on activity.
4. Explanation Activity: Participants learn about what they have been doing and what is known about the topic they have just explored from a presenter, video, demonstration, reading, etc. (Please note that learning while doing comes before learning about something.)
5. Application Activity: Participants figure out how the new knowledge, ideas, or information relates to them. They think about, try out and hone new practices and ideas.
6. Evaluation Activity: Participants clarify the outcomes they are working toward, the meaningfulness of them, and assess their progress.

---

progresses through these important phases of learning by considering activities such as those on the next page.

Here are some questions that can guide you as you design your meeting:

1. Are the activities consistent with the outcomes for the meeting?
2. What atmosphere or context do you need to create for the activities to work?
3. Who needs to participate in which kinds of activities?
4. How will you involve participants in designing the meeting's activities?
5. Will activities work within the time constraints of the meeting?
6. What type of facilities and equipment will the activities require?

Below and in Table 3.1 are 25 different methods and activities for engaging participants in learning. As you design the activities for your meeting, choose a variety to meet diverse needs within your meeting.

- Break-Out Sessions
- Carousel Brainstorming
- Case Study
- Commitment Statements
- Consensus Decision Making
- Demonstrations
- Dialogue and Discussion
- Ground Rules
- Fishbowl
- Group Reflection
- Ice Breakers
- Interview
- Observers
- Panel Presentation
- Poster Sessions/Exhibitions
- Product Development
- Questioners
- Readings
- Review/Reflection Worksheet
- Seasonal Partners
- Simulations
- Small Group Activities/Exercises
- Speech/Formal Presentation
- Use of Video
- Write a "Think Piece"
-

View of Participants in the Design

In a recent meeting, we heard from an accomplished science teacher and school head who said, "I have been attending workshops and conferences for 37 years. I've come to expect the presenter or facilitator to have everything mapped out and to tell me what I am going to do. Recently, I attended a meeting and was asked at the beginning what I wanted to learn and focus on and what role I would play. After I got over the shock, I thought of and shared the questions I had about the topic and worked with a group of other teachers who were interested in learning similar things. I felt responsible for my own learning and guess what? I learned a lot!" As meeting designers we often focus too much on making sure that a leader or presenter has a plan, and too little on the role the participants will play in the plan. If true learning is going to happen in the meetings and conferences, the participants need to have a role that lets them take responsibility for their learning.

This view is shared by leading professional developers in education. Sparks and Hirsch (1997) describe a paradigm shift in staff development in

(text continued on page 40)

TABLE 3.1 25 Conference Learning Activities

Activity	Purpose	Example
Break-out Sessions Small groups meet after a general session to engage with the ideas and concepts presented in the general session. The groups are guided by facilitators or through written instructions. Ideally, break-out sessions produce feedback, ideas, or products that explicitly address the topics of the general session.	To lead participants to reflect and apply the content of the general session.	After a large group lecture or presentation, participants are organized into small groups of 6-10. They have three tasks: (1) to generate the issues that were raised for them by listening to the lecture; (2) to identify the 2-3 key points of learning from the lecture; and (3) to list the implications of the information for them professionally.
Carousel Brainstorming A technique often used when groups are brainstorming lists related to different topics. To increase efficiency and share information with a large group.	To generate many ideas about topics and to increase the likelihood that everyone participates in brainstorming.	At a meeting of educational leaders, one outcome was to generate actions that various groups could take to improve services to children in urban schools. Flipchart paper was placed around the room and labeled with the names of various groups (e.g., social workers, teachers, parents). Each participant started with the group they knew the most about and worked with the others to generate a list of actions. Then the groups traveled to each list reviewing what was there and adding to it.
Case Study Individuals read or view (on videotape) a case study and discuss its key elements, what it teaches, and its relevancy to the group members' own situations.	To learn from the experiences of others in similar or related situations, and to plan changes in one's own practice.	A group of teachers led by a facilitator read a case study of a classroom with specific questions in mind (e.g., how does the teacher use questioning strategies?). They discuss the case, think about what they would do, and relate the case to their own teaching experiences.

Commitment Statements

This is a technique that helps groups focus on what they will do next. Groups are given stem statements like, "We are committed to . . ." and they fill in the blanks and report to the large group or at tables if the group is too large.

To clarify who will do what by when and to be explicit about who has responsibility for taking any next steps.

At a national conference, local teams attended different sessions as individuals then spent a half-day at the end of the conference integrating what they had learned and then decided what next steps to take. At the end, each team stated, "Upon our return, we are committed to doing _____. We will communicate our plans with _____. The outcomes we expect are _____."

Consensus Decision Making

A facilitator elicits the participants' differing views and the strength to which they hold them. The discussion is led to an acceptable consensus position.

To engage a group in making a public decision in which all members let their opinions be known. The group seeks out differences of opinion and acceptable alternatives.

Many groups use the "Fist of Five" approach to consensus. After the group brainstorms ideas and discusses different opinions, a proposal is put forth. Members "vote" with their hands. Five fingers raised indicate total agreement and support for the proposal. Four fingers indicate that the person thinks it is a good solution and they agree to go with it. Three fingers raised indicate the person is willing to go along and support the idea. Two fingers raised indicate the person does not agree with the proposal and will not support it but they will not work against it either. One finger raised indicates the person will actively work against the proposal.

Demonstration

Participants observe an experienced person who shows how to use a product or technique. The demonstrator describes the whys of what he or she does and gives participants the chance to ask questions and learn from the demonstration.

To model effective use of a product or process.

For technology and media use, the presenter leads a small group of people through the use of a program by using a projection screen. Participants watch, raise questions, or comment as the presenter moves through the program.

31

TABLE 3.1 Continued

Activity	Purpose	Example
Dialogue and Discussion There are two forms of discourse that are essential for effective interaction in meetings. Dialogue is divergent and characterized by the group's arguing gracefully to explore alternative ideas departing from a particular viewpoint. Discussion is convergent and characterized by ideas coming together and to closure.	Using both forms of discourse encourages the careful examination of ideas before deciding on actions.	Garmston & Wellman (1998) describe effective teams as those that balance dialogue and discussion. They describe each practice this way: *Dialogue* • Different views are presented as a way of discovering a new perspective • Free and creative exploration of complex, subtle issues • A deep listening • A suspending of one's views • Deepens *understanding* *Discussion* • Different views are presented and defended in search of the best view to support a decision • Analyze and dissect an issue from many points • Winning is usually the goal (one's view prevails) but must take second priority to coherence and truth • Decisions are made
Ground Rules Participants and facilitators establish rules they will adhere to during the meeting.	To create clear expectations and to encourage all to take responsibility for the meeting.	At the start of working together, a group at a national education research center set these ground rules for their meetings: "They who do the work do the learning." "Take care of your own personal needs." "Start and end on time." "Listen and seek first to understand one another." "No question is silly." "Come prepared." As needed they review and revise their ground rules. The latest addition? "Have food at all meetings!"

Fishbowl

Group has focused discussion or dialogue directed by a facilitator. Observation group sits around them and observes for specific things.

To promote active listening, synthesize information, or provide feedback to others.

At a meeting of college professors, five college freshmen engaged in a discussion about the introductory biology and chemistry courses they had recently completed. Professors sat around and listened. The conversation was an exciting counterpoint to prior faculty discussions where they had reviewed research on cooperative learning. The fishbowl discussion brought students' real experiences to bear on the meeting. The fishbowl took place in the evening of day one of a two-day meeting. It not only illustrated points that had been made in other activities but also deepened the second day's discussions.

Group Reflection

Activity to stop the action and have teams reflect on how they are working together.

To improve collaboration and team work and keep group work moving forward productively.

The project managers of a large systemic reform initiative end each of their meetings with these questions:

- How well are we doing at focusing our conversation on one topic at a time?
- Are we following our group ground rules?
- Are we understanding each other?
- What improvements do we need?

TABLE 3.1 Continued

Activity	Purpose	Example
Ice Breakers Activity designed to set the tone of the meeting or conference. They often include a way for participants to introduce and say something about themselves. Ideally, ice breakers engage participants in the subject matter or focus of the meeting—they are not just "fluff."	To create a comfortable atmosphere for the meeting, activate participants' prior knowledge about the subject of the meeting, and assess what people already know or think about a particular topic.	At the National Academy for Science and Mathematics Education Leadership, facilitators began the meeting by spreading evocative black and white photographs (on postcards) out on a table and asking participants to choose a card that suggests a lesson they have learned about leadership. Each person selected a card and then introduced themselves, showed their cards and told the group their "lesson" about leadership. The facilitators wrote the lessons on chart paper and used the list to begin a discussion on what the group knew about leadership. This activity was effective because it let participants reflect on their own prior experience, was directly related to the subject of the meeting, and used visuals to draw out creativity.
Interview Interviewer asks questions of a presenter to draw out key points and ideas. The interviewer often takes questions from the audience, too.	To gain insights from a presenter without listening to one voice for a long time and to tailor a presentation, to address a varied audience's questions and concerns.	At a strategic planning meeting, different role groups were chosen to interview the school superintendent, teachers, and principals. Interviewers included parents, students, teachers, central office personnel, and community members. They asked questions from the perspective of their role group about the vision of the school district and areas for improvement. This process ensured that different perspectives were reflected in the deliberations about strategic goals for the district.

	Description	Purpose	Example
Observers	Participants are designated to observe a meeting or session at a conference and to provide feedback and summary statements during the meeting.	To encourage deeper reflection on the content and process of a meeting and to gain feedback on what is working and what is not. Also to gather information for the meeting evaluation.	Each week one person on staff takes responsibility for being the observer of the staff meeting. They note the flow of the agenda, participation, group dynamics, and lead the staff in reflecting on their observations at the end of each meeting.
Panel Presentation	Several knowledgeable persons talk in response to questions or a guiding topic, often from different perspectives. The focus of the comments is discussed and negotiated before the conference. A moderator provides an overall summary and fields questions from the audience.	To share different perspectives, approaches, or experiences about a topic.	For a forum organized by a national research institute, the design committee decided it was essential to have a panel that was well coordinated and made some key points. The committee invested in preparing panelists. A staff coordinator was assigned to each panel and established a schedule for preparation activities. On a conference call, the panelists developed a general outline of the comments and considered which panelist could best make each point. Panelists produced a 2-5 page briefing paper for advance distribution to participants. This process made panelists more on target, allowed participants to think ahead of time about the key points, and also enabled the coordinators to serve effectively as moderators during the panels.
Poster Sessions/Exhibits	People are invited to set up displays of their resources, products, and work. Displays can include posters, brochures, pictures, student work, video, and computer displays. Participants visit each poster session, view the materials, and talk with the poster session leaders to develop awareness of their work.	To introduce participants to resources and products related to the meeting's topics.	At a national conference, organizers could not provide sufficient room in the agenda for more panelists but wanted to be sure to take advantage of the participants' experiences. They set up a room for participants to display their work and products. To create time in the packed agenda, organizers extended lunch to 90 minutes, provided food, and urged participants to use the lunch period to interact with poster presenters.

TABLE 3.1 Continued

Activity	Purpose	Example
Product Development Work group develops a product that draws upon the different perspectives and expertise in the group.	Bring people together to produce work they could not do alone.	Teams of educators representing teachers, principals, parents, and students come together to develop a school. They clarify their task, decide what success will look like (e.g., outcome indicators), assign roles, and set up a meeting schedule. (Other examples would be using a similar process to develop a product such as a professional development plan or a curriculum guide.)
Questioners Participants are designated to raise questions to presenters/leaders from a particular perspective. For example, a leader presenting a new mathematics curriculum might have someone raise questions from the point of view of an administrator, a parent, a teacher, and a student.	To provoke discussion and learning about how new ideas and materials would work in practice. To raise and address implementation concerns.	In a recent meeting of a state board of education, questioners went through the audience collecting index cards with "burning questions" about some new controversial state policies. Using questioners helped to create a safer environment for asking tough questions.
Readings Prior to the conference or meeting, participants receive readings to prepare them for the meeting. During a conference, readings can be used as a small-group activity. This is often done using a cooperative learning technique called the *jigsaw*—a process through which small-groups are formed and individuals in the group are each given a piece (as in a jigsaw puzzle) of the reading which they then teach to the group.	For reading assigned prior to the meeting, the purpose is to engage the participants in thinking about the conference content beforehand and build a common knowledge base among participants. Readings during the meeting are to build knowledge and have participants engage with the meeting content.	Meeting participants are assigned a section of reading. They read it and make note of the key points. Then they teach the key points about their assignment to the others in their meeting. Collectively, the group discusses the implications of what they read for their situations.

Review/Reflection Worksheet A one- or two-page sheet with blocks for people to record: • What they learned • Insights • Applications	To summarize learning and record actions people think they may take.	After each information session at a national conference, participants returned to the Review/Reflection Worksheet and recorded their insight, learning, and ideas for action. They used the completed form to share ideas with their colleagues during team-meeting time.
Seasonal Partners A technique for getting people to talk with others about what they are learning and thinking (Garmston & Wellman, 1998).	To organize reflection groups for use throughout the meeting and to get people talking with different people at the meeting.	At the beginning of many meetings, we ask participants to make an appointment with four different people—one for each season of the year. We give them a record sheet with a symbol for each season and a place to record the name of the person with whom they will meet. At different points during the meeting we say, "Find your spring (or summer or fall or winter) buddy and reflect on . . . "
Simulations Participants are engaged in a simulated experience—often using real-life situations in computer- or text-based activities. The experience is debriefed to derive learning and generate ideas for practice.	Provide hands-on experience in a reduced-risk environment, often with coaching and feedback.	Participants engage in an inquiry or problem-solving experience that resembles one they would use on the job, such as teachers conducting a scientific investigation that they will facilitate with their own students.

37

TABLE 3.1 Continued

Activity	Purpose	Example
Small Group Activities/Exercises Small groups use instructions or handouts to lead themselves through exercises that might involve answering questions, writing and sharing their ideas with a partner, or generating lists of ideas in the group.	To deepen learning by having participants reflect on information and expand their understanding of it. Also can promote interaction and more in-depth engagement with the content of meeting.	For a conference intended to develop better problem solving strategies, small groups of participants are given a problem statement such as "X% of children in the Shadyside District are achieving below grade-level in reading." Using a problem-solving guide, the small group identifies the data and information they need to clarify the problem, propose possible causes of the problem, and decide how they will design a solution. They present their results to the other small groups.
Speech/Formal Presentation A (mostly) one-way speech or lecture that may involve some questioning of the presenter by the participants. These sessions are enhanced by use of visuals, video or other technology, and humor. The most effective are usually focused on a few key points and limited in length. A way to extend the value of speeches is to have discussants comment on the speech from different points of view. Further, the value and meaningfulness of the speech can be enhanced by combining a speech with a break-out session where participants discuss what the speech meant to them and draw implications for action.	To share a common message or set of ideas with all participants. To hear from leading experts and establish credibility of your message or ideas.	A recent statewide conference on technology planning involved many different sessions that demonstrated technology applications and gave participants planning assistance. A speech was used at the beginning of the day to introduce participants to the "big picture." A highly regarded education technology expert presented the key ideas that needed attention, the overall goals for technology education, and a framework for an overall technology strategy. The speech was effective because it provided participants with background information they needed, gave them a framework to organize the sessions they would attend, and provided experience-based guidance on which they could draw.

Use of Video

Participants view video to learn from examples of practice or presentations from experts on a subject. The video may also be used to provoke thinking about a subject. Facilitator helps viewers by telling them what they will see and by establishing some guidelines for the viewing.

To learn from visual examples and to establish common understanding of what a practice looks like in action; also to see and hear from leading experts without bringing them to your meeting.

A teacher development project is conducting meetings with teachers to examine teaching practices in the classroom. Teachers view video and discuss what they see, what they would do differently, and what they can learn from the example. The facilitator leads the teachers through the same activity they see on the video before they view it so they understand the background and context. The group chooses focus areas for discussion, such as how the students are engaged, and have an observation sheet that they fill out while viewing the video.

Write a "Think Piece"

Participants reflect on a presentation they just heard or react to questions or other prompts. They write what they think and summarize it for other participants.

To get participants to reflect on what they already know, or to generate and document knowledge from participants.

The NISE Forum uses "Think Pieces" after major presentations. Working in small groups participants generate writing about the key points, the issues the presentation raised for them, the questions they have, or how what they heard is relevant to them. Writings are shared and summarized in the small groups. The group reaches consensus on the three or four key points for the meeting record and these are written and submitted to the conference organizers.

which teachers must be involved as learners and have opportunities to reflect critically on their own practices—not just keep adding more and more innovations to their plate. Designing meetings with this view of the participant creates very different outcomes. Vaill (1996) suggests that to survive in the white water world we live in, with all its continuous change, we need to embrace *learning as a way of being.*

Generally this means that all of our activities are focused on learning because it becomes a part of what we do everyday. If you believe that Vaill is right and that we need to change our views of learners as passive recipients of vast knowledge to active self-directed learners, meetings and conferences designed to engage learners need to accommodate such a shift. Self-directed learners have "substantial control over the purposes, the content, the form, and the pace of learning . . . the learner is the primary judge of when sufficient learning has occurred." (1996, p. 58) Few meetings and conferences can make the claim that they work for self-directed learners. One step in the right direction is creating designs with self-directed learning in mind and establishing clear, important, and engaging roles for participants to play as learners at your event. Another is to talk with the presenters and facilitators for your meetings. What is their view of the participants? What role do they think they should play in the meeting? How can they as the meeting leaders increase the opportunity for participants to be self-directed learners?

The Authentic Task Approach

People working to engage participants in accomplishing real work during meetings could look to the Authentic Task Approach (ATA) for a tried and true method (Donohue, Dunne, & Phlegar, 1999). The ATA has eight defined steps:

1. Clarify the task

2. Develop criteria for success

3. Establish a record of work

4. Identify relevant resources

5. Establish group rules and the role of the facilitator

6. Take time to reflect

7. Schedule activities

8. Develop a plan to implement the task

The essence of meetings designed around the ATA is that the participants decide what authentic piece of their work they will do while they are at the meeting, and what the specific outcome will be. Typically, participants in ATA sessions work in teams with people who share a common task. A facilitator usually works with the team to lead them through the eight steps listed above. This "come with a problem, leave with a product" approach is very rewarding. Participants accomplish something that is their real work and do it with the input of a team, the guidance of a facilitator, and help from the many people and material resources assembled at the meeting.

The ATA steps lead participants through a planning and implementation cycle. Steps 1-3 help clarify the team's product. The team generates answers to these questions: What are we going to work on? What will success look like? How will we document our progress? Then the team members move to Step 4, identifying and reviewing relevant resources that the meeting planners bring together for them. For example, for a meeting on leadership development, we collected hundreds of books, print materials, and videotapes and made them available to our participants as they worked through their leadership development tasks. They took surveys to assess their skills, learned leadership development models, and viewed video to see effective leaders in action. As they work together in the early steps of ATA, participants develop collaboration skills. To permit them to continue collaborating, team members may make a commitment to working together after the creation of the product and conclusion of the meeting. In Step 5, the team sets up their own rules of operating and negotiates with their facilitator the role they wish him or her to play. This may change over the course of their work together. Step 6 ensures that team members are continually reflecting on what they have done, the progress made, and where they need to go next. According to the developer of the process, "It's the glue that binds together the various parts of the ATA process" (Donahue, Dunner, & Phlegar, 1999, p. 7). The last steps of the process—scheduling what they will do and developing a plan—assure that the team members will return to their site with a clear sense of the next steps and a commitment to take them.

Using ATA for a meeting or conference requires a *lot* of up-front planning. Ideally, you will know what the teams are coming to work on so you can have the right print and human resources available for them to use. Consider these important pre-meeting activities:

1. Recruit teams who will work together on a real task from their local site

2. Have teams identify a group problem before they arrive at the meeting

3. Assign facilitators who have some expertise about the problem the group wishes to solve

4. Gather relevant resources and make them available throughout the meeting

5. Have computers, printers, Internet connections, and other resources to support teams to produce their product by the end of the meeting

Choosing and Supporting Speakers

If speakers are an important element of your program, then be thorough in selecting and preparing them. If you are using a keynote speaker, choose someone who is knowledgeable, lively, commands the respect of the audience, and has been seen and heard by members of your staff or other people whose judgment you trust. If planning a panel discussion, arrange for panelists to have a conference call to interact, determine logistics, and build strategies to alleviate the "talking head" syndrome. Take full advantage of the potential of panel sessions by designing an appropriate amount and type of preparation. Putting experts together on a platform will usually produce some interesting comments, even if there wasn't prior preparation. But, there isn't always a coherent relationship among the various comments. If you are aiming for an interactive panel, will the exchanges be conceptually productive or will they be random, discordant, or dominated by one vocal panelist? If you really need to ensure that specific points are covered and want productive interactions, you need to arrange for that to happen!

It is a common temptation to choose speakers who conveniently come to mind rather than "pushing the envelope," developing a longer list of candidates, and carefully considering their pros and cons. Well-known speakers, who are in great demand, can have liabilities as well as assets—especially if it is critical to your overall program design for speakers to tailor their remarks or written comments to set up the substance of other activities in the conference. Most busy speakers find it difficult to make time for preparing a presentation that differs much from their standard speeches or to write an advance paper for your event rather than distribute one they already have on hand. You should explore whether it will be possible for them to do this for your conference at the time of your initial request; don't spring preparation tasks on them after the fact. Some of the more recognized experts may be unable to make specific preparations, yet you may go after them anyway because often high-profile experts are needed to help draw participants to your event. The best decisions in these situations are not clear-cut. Weigh the pros and cons of the situation before deciding how to proceed.

To optimize the chances of having your speakers deliver the best possible presentation, be sure to take care of their practical needs so they can focus on preparing for and delivering the substance of the presentation. If your budget permits, offer an honorarium. Be sure they have a hotel reservation. Tell them exactly where to ship any necessary materials in advance and be sure that they have received them upon their arrival at the hotel. Find out whether they need you to obtain any scientific or other supplies locally. Don't let them have to be the ones who find out at some point in their presentation that some audiovisual equipment is not working. If at all possible, do a "dry run" before and encourage your presenters to rehearse any new presentations and get feedback.

We could list a dozen more items to pay attention to. The key is to put yourself in the presenters' shoes—anticipate their needs and support their efforts. There is a small but frustrating hazard to avoid that we found in our work with some scientists and mathematicians: the overhead transparency or slide with impossibly small characters. Fortunately, with electronic preparation of audiovisuals taking over the field, this problem is disappearing. However, we still see presentations where this happens. Your audience will benefit if you can find a way to preview your presenters' audiovisuals in advance to ensure they are readable and polished.

Communicate With Leaders, Facilitators, and Presenters

Send letters to all leaders, facilitators, and presenters to confirm their participation. Document the expectations you have for their work at the meeting. Follow up the mailing with a phone call or e-mail message to review the conference expectations, discuss plans to ensure quality, engaging sessions, and to address any questions or problems.

Depending on the guidelines for your organization, you may also need to send all leaders or presenters a contract detailing the financial arrangements you have negotiated with each of them, which must be signed by them and returned to you prior to the conference. Check in with them again prior to the conference to confirm travel arrangements and other logistics. Consider meeting or holding a conference call with all presenters before your event.

There is quite a bit of information that should be obtained from and/or provided to your meeting leaders or facilitators. Complete contact information is essential including e-mail addresses. There are a lot of other information needs that are easy to overlook. Make sure you have the following:

- Title of session
- Type of session (simulation, discussion, etc.)
- Brief description of session content (paragraph or more)
- Brief description of session methods/techniques (phrases or sentences)
- Target audience, experience (none, some, very knowledgeable)
- Target audience, type (mathematicians, mathematics ed. specialists, teachers, etc.)
- Brief description of the outcomes participants will gain
- Previous history of making this or similar presentation (yes/no)
- Special requirements for room setup or audiovisual
- Permission for taping (audio and/or video)
- Permission to publish any papers in conference proceedings

Market the Conference

Depending on the number and kinds of people you are recruiting to your meeting, you may need a low- or high-level marketing effort. If you have cosponsors who have members or constituencies, work with them to send notices of the meeting to all of their members. If you are recruiting large numbers of people, you may also consider placing paid advertisements or free announcements in professional associations' newsletters. (We have used wide-reaching publications such as *Education Week* for this purpose.)

If you have a website, post the invitation there. It is quickly becoming easier and less expensive than it was initially to permit participants to register via the Web. Be warned, however, that at this time, you still also will have to permit registration by mail. There are plenty of people who do not engage in these functions electronically even when they have the capability. For a recent NISE Forum that targeted higher education faculty and administrators in science and mathematics, we received four mail registrations for every Web registrant, even though most of the target audiences had ready access to the Web.

The most popular and highest yielding strategy is to mail the meeting announcement to an identified audience and to follow up with targeted phone calls to recruit key people. This approach is also recommended for small meetings. Some organizations will provide you with mailing lists for their membership. These lists can range in cost from zero to hundreds of dollars. If possible, encourage people to come in teams so they can meet with their coworkers and determine how best to use the information back home; if you are charging a registration fee, you can offer a reduced rate for two people from the same organization.

If you cannot put a lot of effort into marketing, you may want to explore bringing your meeting to another existing meeting. We have done this by scheduling a meeting one day before the start of the annual or regional meetings of the national mathematics and science associations. This strategy allows you to draw people who will already be traveling to the site, thereby tapping into a ready-made audience and limiting additional travel costs. All associations are different; contact the ones you work with to find out how you can add your meeting to their conferences.

Just before the meeting, prepare a press release that participants can send to local media outlets. If this is a larger conference, contact the education and/or science and mathematics writers at the area newspaper, provide them with a copy of the press release and invite them to the meeting. Publicity can draw others to your future conferences and you can also copy press articles to send as follow-up to your participants.

Prepare Pre-Conference Participant Mailings

As people register for your conference, it is a good idea to gather some information about them and to reinforce that the conference stays on their agenda. We recommend doing two pre-conference mailings. Very early, send a post card or short one-pager confirming registration. Include the highlights of the meeting, the location, and contact information. Send out a second mailing including a participant survey gathering information on conference expectations and assess special needs, such as food or physical space requirements. Also, send an agenda book or conference packet including the schedule, detailed directions, site information, and any reading that participants are expected to do ahead of the meeting. If you have the time and budget to provide a draft participant list in advance, attendees appreciate being able to get a sense of the kinds of people they will be joining. They can identify people they already know and want to be sure to see, as well as people they might want to meet for the first time.

Websites, electronic discussion groups, and e-mail present a great opportunity for conference and meeting planners. These technologies support both pre- and post meeting activities. For example, the EdGateway system operated by WestEd registers meeting participants online, creates a database of the sessions people wish to attend, organizes discussion groups for the conference itself, and sets up post-conference messaging for follow-up. Another group, the Coalition of Essential Schools, asks meeting presenters to submit their session proposals on the EdGateway system. They are reviewed on line and feedback is generated to presenters. Such new cutting-edge developments in interactive web-based software addresses the challenge of collecting, organizing, and disseminating information. You can enter information about your organizations or your events and have them posted thereby helping with the advertising of your event.

Many people are experimenting with online communities as a means to follow up on conversations started during conferences and to build networks before, during, and after the meetings. This is still fairly uncharted territory for most of us. Through our work with a national leadership academy, we have learned that most people need some form of moderator to sustain online communication. Additionally, technology that groups the comments and ideas that relate to one another or "threads" the conversations seems to help people get in on and follow the conversations better. Many web-based systems set up places for group conversation and send the message to people's e-mail addresses, eliminating the need to check two sites for messages. These developments will help to eliminate some of the barriers to good online discussions and make this a more viable way to interact with participants in the future.

Manage the Conference

The day before your event, check all of the rooms you will use the next day. Figure 3.1 is a sample checklist for inspecting meeting rooms.

Check that the rooms are set up the way you or your presenters requested. Ask about the schedule for delivering AV equipment to the rooms and check where it will be placed. If the room is secure, set up any displays and/or participant materials. Identify the various entrances that participants could use to enter the building and be sure there are many signs for your meeting or some other device that directs them to the right rooms

Figure 3.1. Room Checklists

General Checks: **Room:** _____   **Session:** _____

_____   easel with plenty of newsprint
_____   markers (at least three different colors)
_____   masking tape
_____   water pitcher on side table and plenty of glasses (appropriate
                       number for the size of the room)
_____   the room is clean: no material leftover from previous group
_____   chairs are pushed in at the tables
_____   tablecloths are clean
_____   notepads and pencils are at every seat in rectangular tables or at
                       the center of the table, if round

Specific Checks

What AV equipment needs to be in the room?

_____
_____
_____

What should the room arrangement be?

_____
_____
_____

What material should be there?

_____
_____
_____

(e.g., assign staff to direct participants). This is often a problem in large facilities such as those at colleges where there is no obvious lobby or information source, like the front desk in a hotel, and there are many entrances to the building. Confirm whether your facility has posted your event on signs or electronic marquees as you had planned. Make arrangements to have at least one staff member greet and register all participants and assign another staff to make sure rooms, presenters, and materials are in order.

If they have not been mailed ahead of time, conference notebooks or folders and nametags must be given out when participants arrive. Arrange nametags in alphabetical order in an indexed box. The notebooks or folders should have the agenda on the front for easy reference. Handouts from all sessions should be included or available at the registration desk, as well as a list of all participants, their addresses, e-mail and fax numbers.

Bring a conference organizer's toolkit: rubber bands, paper clips, large metal clamps, scissors, stapler with staples, three-way wall plug, grounded adapter unit, masking tape, packages of "post-its," map pins, nametags, water-based markers, scotch tape, transparencies, transparency markers, newsprint, felt markers, etc.

It is also a good idea to have a staff member attend each session as a resource person for the presenter. These resource people can observe and collect data, as well as be there to help solve problems that might come up with equipment, the room, or the participants. Assign a staff member to each presenter so that he or she knows to whom to go for help.

Be sure you know how to contact the engineering and audiovisual departments to adjust environmental conditions and AV equipment as needed. Another way to provide support at your conference is to have a resource room of books, articles, curriculum, and other materials that participants may want to use during the conference. If you do this, people may want to make copies to take home; if possible, set up a copy service or send materials to participants after the conference. Alternatively, find out what business services are offered by the site.

For larger meetings, someone must be designated to make sure the hotel or conference center provides all agreed-on services in an acceptable way, especially if this is your first time at the location. You should not assume that the site will perform according to plan because, unfortunately, even the best properties may let you down now and then. During a recent NISE Forum, we discovered that one hour prior to a break-out session, the designated ballroom was completely empty instead of containing 30 tables with tablecloths, chairs and water service, as specified on the hotel's function sheet for our conference! Admittedly, you should not have to make sure the hotel is doing its job. If something goes wrong, however, it will be your participants who are inconvenienced. So, in advance of every element of your program, be sure everything is going according to plan.

Attending to the myriad details as well as providing a substantial and worthwhile meeting is a huge undertaking. As you plan your meeting, be sure that you have the people and resources to cover all of the bases discussed above. If not, you may want to hire outside help, such as product development, secretarial services, or even a conference planner. Otherwise, consider scaling back your plans. When you and your staff begin to tire of the tedious and thankless practical arrangements, remember that these steps are critical to creating good learning conditions. Every distraction that participants experience due to lack of good design or execution takes away from their ability to concentrate on the substance of your meeting or conference. Every problem avoided increases the chances of gaining the outcomes and products you need.

4

Evaluating Your
Conference or Meeting

I n the planning stages of a conference or meeting, we suggested that conference and meeting designers should think carefully before they decide to invest the resources to conduct an effective event. In this chapter, we suggest that you find out how well your investment has paid off by measuring your success. Although most people know they need to build some evaluation activity into meetings and conferences, they rarely go beyond measuring how happy participants were with the experience. We encourage you to design evaluation activities that measure *both* participant satisfaction *and* the outcomes of the meeting.

Focus of the Evaluation

There are two major questions that the evaluation of your meeting and conference should address: (1) did the meeting produce the desired outcomes and (2) were the participants' expectations met? Your primary focus should be assessing whether the outcomes and purposes of your meeting were met. Keep in mind that the outcomes should have a direct benefit for the participants—not just benefit you or your program.

The first step to evaluation is to clarify your goals or purposes. What results do you expect from your conference or meeting? Your outcome statements should be *SMART*: *S*pecific, *M*easurable, *A*ttainable, *R*elevant, and *T*imely (Ramsborg, 1995, pp. 64-74).

Specific—each goal should be clear, concise, and in active voice
Measurable—you can identify and assess each goal's indicators of success
Attainable—you can accomplish the goal with the strengths, abilities, and resources you have
Relevant—there is a documented need for and interest in your goal
Timely—your goals are not too complex for the available time

Outcomes should be a statement of the impact that will result from your efforts (e.g., to improve teaching and learning of science). Good outcome statements are often hard to formulate because many of us confuse activities (such as "hold a meeting" or "conduct a training session") with real outcomes (e.g., develop deep understanding of physical science among K-3 teachers and students in my school).

As you generate outcomes for meetings, ask yourself, "what will it look like if I am successful?" For example, if your overall goal is to implement an improved science curriculum in your school, one outcome of your meeting could be that all of the teachers are aware of the new curriculum and understand the next steps for implementation. Another outcome might be that a group of teachers take on a leadership role to address implementation problems and look for ways to help their colleagues use the new curriculum. Notice the outcomes are not that teachers get a copy of the new curriculum or that they attend training; but rather, good outcome statements will reflect what happens as a result of the meeting or conference.

Next consider whether the event you have planned can realistically achieve the expected outcomes. Use data you have gathered from your participants through a pre-conference survey or from a design committee to be sure that the outcomes you have stated are meaningful to your participants.

Identify the Audience for the Evaluation

Your evaluation effort should gather the right data for the right audiences. Typically you will want to report what you learn to participants, staff, co-workers, and funders. Think about what these people want to know. Funders may be interested in knowing how many people were contacted, as well as the results of the data gathered. Staff may be more interested in knowing the areas of the event that went well and those that need to be re-thought. Staff and presenters need to hear specific feedback on their presentations so they can make improvements next time. Participants may want to know how others rated their experience and to get a sense of how people may be thinking about applying the topic of the meeting. Addressing these different information needs should be a part of your plan.

Consider who your primary audience is for the evaluation. What do they want to know? Are they more interested in "counting beans"—knowing how many people from what role groups were reached—or are they interested in the results participants achieved? Then consider what you want to know. Think about information that will help you become more effective. Focus your data collection plan on gathering the information to help you improve and to satisfy the needs of your primary audiences.

Choose Data Collection Methods

Good evaluation starts with the ability to ask good questions. Review your outcome statements and think about how these can be measured. What questions would you ask? What data or evidence would show that you achieved your outcomes? Outcomes such as increasing interest or awareness of a particular idea or topic can be measured by asking questions on a pre- or post-survey about new information that participants have gained as a result of the session. Depending on your outcomes, you will use different data collection and measurement strategies. Below and in Figure 4.1, we highlight some common outcomes and the types of evaluation methods that can be used to measure them (Loucks-Horsley et al., 1987).

Figure 4.1. Methods of Documentation and Measurement for Different Outcome Types

	Pre-/Post-Measures	Surveys	Observations	Interview	Document Review
Changes in participant knowledge	X	X			
Changes in participant skill level		X	X	X	X
Changes in participant opinions or beliefs		X		X	
Changes in organizational capacity		X	X	X	
Changes in student achievement	X	X	X	X	X

SOURCE: Loucks-Horsley et al., 1987.

Changes in participants. Conferences and meetings often aim to promote some change in the participants' knowledge, skills, opinions, and/or beliefs. What changes do you expect from your activity? To measure changes in knowledge use pre- and post-testing, surveys, and interviews. To assess growth in skill level, observe participants as they demonstrate the skill, use a self-assessment checklist that asks participants to rate their skill level, or conduct interviews. If you expect changes in opinions or beliefs, you can gather evidence from listening to people's comments at the beginning and end of the meeting. Ask open-ended questions that get participants to share their ideas and views about a subject at the beginning of the meeting and document their statements. At the end of the meeting, return to the list to see what people would add or change as a result of their experience in the meeting.

Changes in organization. Rarely will one conference or meeting result in organizational changes unless the meeting involves a critical mass of people from the organization (Bolman & Deal, 1992). If this is the case, however, changes in the organization can result—they may just not show up right away. If your meeting is intended as a means to make organizational changes, be specific about the expected change (e.g., putting continuous improvement processes in place, conducting ongoing professional development, increasing communication, building collegial networks, developing leadership, or making decisions on the basis of data). If your outcome is to promote networking, you could ask participants who they met, what they learned, and how they might build or maintain relationships forged at the conference. To measure these outcomes, assess the organizational climate—to what extent do attitudes and beliefs reflect the desired outcome? Interview or survey members of the organization to determine the extent to which the change has happened. If possible, conduct the survey several times to gather evidence of changes over time. Observation of staff is also a good method to assess organizational change. Meetings may be aimed at reviewing current policy and making decisions about changes. To assess that the change in policy has been made, you can review documents and survey or interview participants about the change.

Changes in students. Still other events are intended as a means to promote improvements in teaching and learning that benefit students. When change in students is your expected outcome, first gather data on the intentions of the participants in your meeting. What do they intend to do as a result of the conference? If the participants intend to do something different in their work with students, the results of this can be measured by teachers' assessment of students, formal tests, student products or portfolios, surveys, classroom observations, interviews with students or parents, etc. However, no direct cause-effect relationship can be drawn because of other factors at work.

Outcomes that reflect long-term changes are harder to measure at the end of a session. To measure these types of outcomes, gather information about participants' intentions to do something different or to change their practices. To assess whether this really happens would require a follow-up contact later on. One efficient way to do this is to e-mail a short survey to participants 3 to 6 months after your event.

Evaluating the Meeting Design and Process

In addition to gathering evidence about the outcome results, it is also important to evaluate the meeting itself. This part of the evaluation should ask participants about the value and the relevance of the conference to them, the quality of the presenters/leaders, the variety and quality of the design and content presented, and the overall organization of the conference. Ask for ideas for improvements. Review "Characteristics of Effective Meetings and Conferences" in Chapter 1 to formulate questions to assess the meeting design and execution.

Methods for Evaluating the Meeting

Construct an end-of-conference evaluation form that asks questions about the different elements. Your evaluation form might include questions with a Likert scale, such as:

"To what extent was the meeting valuable to you?"

4	3	2	1
Extremely Valuable	Valuable	Somewhat Valuable	Not Valuable

These questions are easy to score but provide little descriptive information. Therefore, it is a good idea to also include some open-ended questions such as, "In what ways was the meeting valuable to you?" or "How will you use what you learned at the meeting in the future?" Resource C provides some sample evaluation forms.

For a multi-day session, gather evaluation data each day and ask participants to complete a final evaluation form on the last day. In lieu of using a daily form, you can put index cards on each table for participants to offer feedback throughout the day. Tape colorful gift bags around the room for people to deposit the cards in. Collect the cards at the end of each day. These can be read aloud by the leaders at the end of the day or the next morning. Also, the leaders should offer their own observations about the day and suggest any changes they might make in subsequent days. Each evening, staff should review the feedback and decide how to respond and report to the full group the next morning.

If follow-up meetings will occur, the evaluation should ask participants what they intend to do between meetings (e.g., with their new knowledge/information/skills). Conference planners can then gather information at subsequent meetings to assess whether participants followed through on their intentions. You can use this information to assess needs for follow-up work and to design it.

Another useful evaluation method is to appoint observers for all the conference sessions. The observers attend the meeting and talk informally with participants about what they are learning, how it is going, and what suggestions they have for improvements. The observers meet at the end of the day or meeting to synthesize their observations and findings. In smaller meetings, the facilitators or leaders can stop the process periodically to have participants reflect on the objectives, what they are learning, whether they are on target for accomplishing their purposes, what they want more (or less of), and to give feedback to the sessions' leaders. This type of ongoing participant feedback is powerful because it involves the participants in shaping the event and helps to establish an environment of continuous learning and improvement. Collecting data becomes a conscious and con-tinuous act embedded in all meetings. These ongoing methods enable lead-ers to know what is working, what isn't and why, and to make necessary adjustments.

Use of Evaluation Information to Make Improvements

Plans for using evaluation data should include ideas for linking feedback to future conferences and for sending any additional follow-up materials to participants, as needed. If you are leading a multi-day event, give a short summary to participants of the evaluation results from the previous day. Describe what the participants reported and tell participants how you will act on the comments for the remaining days and in future meetings. For ex-ample, if the evaluations say that there was too much content and not enough time, tell participants how you will slow down the pace in the sub-sequent days. If the room temperature was uncomfortable, tell them what you have done to fix it. Likewise, if you are meeting with the same group over time, share the evaluation information with them after each meeting and tell them how you will address the feedback. It can also be very pro-ductive to ask participants to help solve a problem that comes out in the evaluation. For example, at a recent meeting, people complained that they didn't have adequate time to meet and network with one another. The agenda was already over-booked and it seemed we could not be responsive to this feedback. A group of participants suggested putting together a gath-ering in the hotel lounge before dinner which resulted in half of the group continuing their networking over dinner.

Conference and meeting leaders should meet during and at the end of the conference to debrief every aspect of the conference. Plan at least an hour after the conference to celebrate the successes and discuss what needs improvement. Designate one person to facilitate the session and another person to take detailed notes. This is especially important when the conference will be repeated again. Review the evaluation forms. What did the participants say about their experience? If you have a large group, take a sample of the forms to read aloud. If the evaluations show that there were sessions that were unsuccessful, discuss what went wrong and how you might change them in the future. If sessions were well received, what factors made them so and how could you build more of these factors into other sessions?

Step back from the particulars and look at the overall conference. What would you do differently next time? How was participation? If you had 200 people at the meeting, what were your numbers during break-out sessions? Did people participate or leave? Why? For example, if meetings lack time for networking, people will often use break-out session time for that purpose. Did certain people dominate and if so what was done to address this? How were the presenters/leaders? Did they do what they were asked to do? Did they achieve their objectives? What feedback do you have for them? What would you want them to do differently next time?

It can be hard to receive negative feedback, but with the help of participant evaluation forms and the observations of others, the debriefing period can be a good time for reflection and learning. Set up your debriefing session in a safe environment for learning and improvement—not blaming and finger-pointing. If particular sessions were not well received, ask, what was going on? Often the people with the most challenging messages to deliver are met with the most resistance. Was this the case? Was it the message, the messenger, or something else? In assessing meeting effectiveness, it is critical to consider what was going on and who was leading the effort in order to get the full picture.

Regular Evaluation of Small Meetings and Working Sessions

In this chapter, we have presented ideas and information for designing and conducting evaluation activities for larger-scale conferences. We recommend that you also build routine evaluation into staff meetings, working sessions, and other smaller meetings. The methods for gathering evaluation data in smaller settings are easier. Include the outcomes for the meeting on the printed agenda or post them on newsprint. As you start the meeting, review the outcomes with all present and ask for any additional outcomes not reviewed. Take a minute to ask participants what evidence should be considered to determine whether your meeting outcomes have been met. At the end of each part of your agenda, review the outcomes for that part and reflect on what you have accomplished. At the end of the meeting, ask participants to assess how well the outcomes were achieved and offer any suggestions for future meetings.

In summary, recognize the importance of gathering evaluative information about your meeting and its outcomes. Be sure to establish clear outcomes for your event and design the evaluation to measure achievement of those outcomes. Be clear about your audience for the evaluation. You may want to collect some data for in-house consumption and some for outside audiences. Report what you learn from the evaluation verbally at the meeting and in a written summary report. Share your findings with all of your primary audiences; use staff and advisory meetings to review your results and to make improvements in future meetings.

C
H
A
P
T
E
R

5

Producing Conference Proceedings

I t takes a lot of stamina to plan and execute a successful learning event, but there is still another design element that frequently is overlooked or shortchanged—producing a post-conference report or proceedings. This chapter briefly outlines possible uses of proceedings and outlines how to capture what transpires at meetings and conferences. The closing section addresses a commonly missed opportunity—capturing, analyzing, and reporting the valuable ideas advanced by participants during various kinds of small group sessions.

Purposes of Proceedings

Producing a summary of the major points and information presented in your meeting or conference is beneficial for a number of reasons. First, participants in the meeting can refer back to the summary as they try to tell others about their experience or apply what they learned to their own situation. Second, the summary can serve as a report that can be submitted to sponsors or funders for the conference. Third, if you want to build on the conference and perhaps convene other groups similarly, the conference summary document might be used to interest new people in your ideas.

Finally, and most obviously, the document can help provide an overview of the key ideas and information to people who could not attend your event. It extends the reach of your efforts and produces interest among people who may come to future events. For example, the National Institute for Science Education uses its Annual Forum as a means to generate new knowledge in the area of science and mathematics education reform. The conference proceedings capture knowledge that is generated and then makes it available for wider dissemination to people beyond the attendees.

Ways to Capture the Meeting

Although there are many benefits to producing and distributing such a document, it requires a lot of work and front-end planning to make sure you have recorded enough of the conference or meeting information to put together a useful document. Identify the people who will be responsible for the summary document prior to the meeting. These people can come up with a plan to gather as much of the writing and examples for the document before or during the conference, thereby minimizing the work of re-creating events later on. Below are some suggestions for how to build the documents and information you will need to compile a complete and useful summary document.

Identify note-takers. Many people take thorough notes of meetings. Identify ahead of time either staff or a couple of participants to take notes. Agree on a format for the notes, such as summary of ideas, key discussion points, dilemmas raised, and resources suggested. Alternatively, identify the themes you want to report and ask note-takers to synthesize what they learn around the themes. Tell all note-takers that you expect them to spend time reflecting on, thinking through, and writing up a narrative. To get the most out of your notes, pick careful thinkers who can interpret and synthesize information within your note-taking structure, not just act as scribes.

Assign recorders to work with each small group to summarize discussions and key learning. Often some of the richest discussions and insights come within small group activities. These important ideas do not get captured unless people are assigned to synthesize them in some way. Suggest a format for capturing the key points of the discussion. Recorders can document ideas on newsprint or paper and submit them to the conference organizers right after the small group meeting.

Follow up on e-mail. Identify a few participants to follow up with through e-mail after the conference. Send them a message right after the meeting asking them to respond to specific questions or provide thoughts, new ideas, learnings, or ask questions that were provoked by their experience during the meeting. In addition to helping you by providing material for the conference proceedings, you will be encouraging them to reengage with the topics of your conference and to think about how their experience at the conference can contribute to their own work.

Ask presenters to prepare papers. Many meeting leaders prepare their ideas and comments in writing prior to a conference or meeting so they can be circulated in advance. Decide on a standard format for all papers and ask presenters to submit them in a form that can be reproduced or edited slightly for inclusion in the conference proceedings document. Build in time and resources to edit the set of papers, to give presenters an opportunity to react to your changes, and to address their feedback. Get copies of overheads and other visuals used by presenters.

Video- or audiotape presentations and photographs. Some conference proceedings include videotapes or audiotapes of actual presentations. For example, a recording of a keynote speaker who sets the tone for the entire conference would be a complement to the printed proceedings. If you decide to use this strategy, be sure to invest in qualified technicians to set up and operate your recording equipment. Audiotaping can also be used to record a presentation that you want to include verbatim or summarize in your proceedings document. Again, be sure that the taping equipment is producing quality sound so that it can be heard clearly and understood. Make transcripts of the presenters and discussants that can be edited and included in the proceedings. If graphics can be included in the summary document, take pictures.

Use the evaluation. Include questions on your evaluation form that will give you good information for your summary document. For example, you might ask participants to write down one or two ideas discussed at the meeting that were particularly useful to them and ask them to describe how they might use this information in their work. Or, ask participants to write a few questions that were provoked for them by their participation in this meeting.

Plan ahead. Assembling all of these artifacts will be easier if you decide ahead of time on a format and an organization of the conference proceedings. Most often, proceedings include summaries or the text of formal presentations, a background piece on the purpose and themes of the meeting, a description of the activities participants engaged in, the participants' comments, insights, and learning, and any products produced during the meeting such as recommendations, plans, models, etc. Appendices such as agendas, handouts, and participant lists are also often included. Decide which of these will be a part of your document and establish a plan for gathering the information you will need for each section prior to the meeting.

Adding Analysis to Reporting

In Chapter 3, we emphasized the importance of being sure to engage participants in discussions. From a perspective of adult learning, participants need occasions to process information in order to understand and adapt it to their current knowledge and circumstances.

Another reason for using activities that engage participants in discussion is to elicit and capture their views for the organizers' purposes. If participants' wisdom would be of benefit to organizers or others, make the effort to systematically collect as much of it as possible. For example, the annual NISE Forums draw a very experienced audience, many of whom are as qualified as the Forum's presenters. Further, the Forum's purpose is to advance the state of knowledge on the topic selected. So, failing to acquire the participants' views would be quite a waste. The previous section discussed designating note takers for discussion sessions, but here we describe a more intensive strategy for documenting a conference.

After each panel session of the NISE Forum, participants are assigned to small groups to debate particulars of what they have heard. During these break-out sessions, all participants are asked to spend about 10-15 minutes writing a "think piece" where they can choose to react to one of several questions which are linked to the previous panel session. Over the course of the Forum's three break-out sessions, the 300 participants produced a total of about 600 written think pieces. Participants also completed a form authorizing Forum organizers to reproduce portions of their think pieces in the Forum proceedings and indicating whether or not to identify the author.

For purposes of creating the Forum proceedings, these think pieces were treated as a *data set of expert opinions* on the important topics discussed at the Forum. A research and evaluation team carefully and exhaustively studied this data set using modern methods of qualitative analysis. As a result, the Forum proceedings could include a credible reporting of the 300 Forum participants' views in addition to presenting standard proceedings' elements such as the panelists' remarks, agenda, and a participant list. Figure 5.1 is an excerpt of the 27-page section of an NISE Forum Proceedings that resulted from such an analysis (Mason, Gunter, Miller, & Seymour, 1998).

Figure 5.1. Analysis and Reporting of Participants' Views

Alignment Within and Between Departments

Writers who focused on alignment issues also noted that the goals of a course be aligned with those of other courses (within and across departments) and that related courses should incorporate common assessment and evaluation strategies. For example, one undergraduate administrator noted the importance of aligning pedagogical methods within multisection courses:

> My concerns as an administrator are threefold. The first is to encourage my departments and faculty to begin to consider the implementation of new (or different) methods of curriculum at the general education and advanced (major) level. Realizing that this normally occurs at a course-by-course level, the next step would be to ensure that multisection/multi-instructor courses employ the same (or similar) evaluation and assessment methods.

Marlene Moore and Cora Marrett explained that students outcomes—skills and content knowledge—should be articulated within and between departments.

> It is critical to remember that none of us work in isolation. If goals for our introductory classes do not fit the expectation of colleagues whose courses build on our course, the assessment by colleagues of our course will be negative. (Moore)

> Goals should be set and articulated for any SMET course. Although course-based goals must exist, goals and assessment should [emerge from] community-wide discussion of intended outcomes for SMET education and articulation of assessment strategies across levels and the curriculum. (Marrett)

A few expressed concerns about whether the implementation of innovative course objectives negatively affects student command of course content needed for subsequent courses. This issue was of particular concern to new faculty:

> I am skeptical when the [new course goals] carry with them changes in course content. Are we certain that the resulting course content doesn't lower the standards of the course, affect the smooth transition into subsequent courses, or [hinder] achievement of the type of scientist/mathematician we desire?

> Nagging Question (probably comes from the background of having students who must possess a certain knowledge base to enter a profession): Where and how does curriculum content (amount, type, level) fit in? I think we should not lose sight of this as we begin to focus on higher level skills.

SOURCE: Reproduced by permission from the National Institute for Science Education (Mason et al., 1998).

Note that the inclusion of an analysis of participants' writings not only increases the authenticity and credibility of the document but also enlivens the reading of it. Although we have seen many conference proceedings include quotes from participants, these often were obtained ad hoc or after the fact and are not necessarily representative of other participants' views. In contrast, the systematic collection and methodical analysis of all participant views described here permits organizers to legitimately claim a more representative portrayal of the participants' wisdom.

Resource A

Examples of Topics Addressed
by Professional Meeting Planners

Budgeting and financial management
Site selection
Promotion, marketing and printing
Housing
Transportation
Food and beverage arrangements
The convention and visitor's bureau
The role of the convention services manager
Negotiations with site
Registration procedures
Audiovisuals
Hospitality, spouse/guest
Contracted services
Legal issues, contracts, and liability
Americans With Disabilities Act

During the Meeting

Speaker arrangements and care

Space use and set-up design

Final instructions

Onsite communications

Onsite emergencies

Meeting wrap-up

Meeting evaluation

Types of Meetings

Alternative meeting environments

Convention centers

Exposition management

Small meeting management

International meetings and expositions

Technology in the meetings industry

Green meetings

The professional meeting manager

Resource B

Sample Agendas

SAMPLE 1: Schedule for a Two-Day Conference

Third Annual NISE Forum: February 23-24, 1998

Renaissance Hotel, Washington, DC, 999 9th Street, NW
(202)898-9000.

Indicators of Success in Postsecondary Science, Mathematics, Engineering
and Technology Education: Shapes of the Future

**Sunday,
February 22**

4:00-7:00	Registration	Foyer, Meeting Room 11

**Monday,
February 23**
Monday sessions on Meeting Room level
(Tuesday sessions on Ball Room Level)

7:30-8:30	Registration continued	Foyer, Meeting Room 11
	Continental breakfast provided	Auditorium Foyer

Opening Session

8:30-9:15	*Welcome, Overview*	Auditorium
	Andrew Porter, National Institute for Science Education	

Neal Lane, National Science Foundation

Shaping the Future   Auditorium

Luther Williams, National Science Foundation

Session One: Assessment of Teaching, Learning, and Curriculum Change in Classrooms

9:15-10:45   **A. Panel Discussion**   Auditorium

　　　　　　Chair: Arthur Ellis, National Institute for Science Education

　　　　　　Facilitator: Brock Spencer, Beloit College

　　　　　　　　Diane Ebert-May, Northern Arizona University

　　　　　　　　Eric Mazur, Harvard University

　　　　　　　　David Porter, U.S. Air Force Academy

　　　　　　Discussant: Norman Fortenberry, National Science Foundation

　　　　　　Forum Data Collection Plan

　　　　　　Susan Miller, National Institute for Science Education

10:45-11:15   *Break, beverages provided*   Foyer, Meeting Rooms
　　　　　　　　　　　　　　　　　　　　　　　　　　2,10

11:15-12:30   **B. Small Group Discussions**   See Name Badge for
　　　　　　　　　　　　　　　　　　　　　　　　　　Group Assignment

　　　　　　Groups Numbered 1-6 convene in Meeting Room 2.

　　　　　　Groups Numbered 7-11 convene in Meeting Room 3.

　　　　　　Groups Numbered 12-16 convene in Meeting Room 4.

　　　　　　Groups Numbered 17-20 convene in Meeting Room 8.

　　　　　　Groups Numbered 21-24 convene in Meeting Room 9.

　　　　　　Groups Numbered 25-27 convene in Meeting Room 10.

　　　　　　Groups Numbered 28-30 convene in Meeting Room 11.

12:30-2:15   *Lunch Provided; networking opportunity*   Foyer, Meeting
　　　　　　　　　　　　　　　　　　　　　　　　　　Room 11

　　　　　　C. Poster Session   Meeting Rooms
　　　　　　　　　　　　　　　　　　　　　　　　　　12-14

Sesssion Two: Assessment and the Promotion of Change in Departments, Disciplines, and Institutions

2:15-4:00   **A. Panel Discussion**   Auditorium

　　　　　　Chair: Robert Mathieu, National Institute for Science Education

　　　　　　Facilitator: Elaine Seymour, University of Colorado-Boulder

Brian Coppola, University of Michigan

Eileen Lob Lewis, Canada College

Richard Taipa, Rice University

Discussant: Daryl Chubin, National Science Foundation

4:00-4:15	*Break, beverages and cookies provided*	Foyer, Meeting Rooms 2,10

4:15-5:30	**B. Small Group Discussants**	See Name Badge for Group Assignment

Groups Numbered 1-6 convene in Meeting Room 2.

Groups Numbered 7-11 convene in Meeting Room 3.

Groups Numbered 12-16 convene in Meeting Room 4.

Groups Numbered 17-20 convene in Meeting Room 8.

Groups Numbered 21-24 convene in Meeting Room 9.

Groups Numbered 25-27 convene in Meeting Room 10.

Groups Numbered 28-30 convene in Meeting Room 11.

Dinner on your own

Tuesday, February 24	All Tuesday sessions on Ballroom level (different level than Monday).	
7:00-8:00	*Contintental breakfast provided*	Foyer, Grand Ballroom North

Session Three: The Role of Evaluation in Institutional and National Policy and Practice

8:00-9:30	**A. Panel Discussion**	Grand Ballroom North

Chair: Ann Burgess, National Institute for Science Education

Facilitator: Clifford Adelman, National Institute for Science Education

Jack Bristol, University of Texas-El Paso

Manuel Gómez, University of Puerto Rico

Sherri Sheppard, Stanford University

Discussant: Larry Suter, National Science Foundation

9:30-9:45	*Break, beverages provided*	Foyer, Grand Ballroom South

9:45-11:00   **B. Small Group Discussions**   See Name Badge for
                                                                 Group Asssignment

Groups Numbered 1-11 convene in Grand Ballroom Central.

Groups Numbered 12-22 convene in Grand Ballroom South.

Groups Numbered 23-30 convene in Congressional B.

Closing Session

11:15-Noon   *Reflection and Synthesis*   Grand Ballroom North

Chair: Andrew Porter

Cora Marrett, University of Massachusetts-Amherst

John Wiley, University of Wisconsin-Madison

Forum Evaluation

SAMPLE 2: Professional Development Conference

Session: Study Groups

Outcomes for the session:

1. Gaining new learning from two papers
2. Experiencing cooperative learning structures that reinforce learning and promote effective teaching practices
3. Experiencing the study group strategy
4. Networking within and among teams

Materials:

- Reading material to be used in the study group
- Written instructions for cooperative learning structures to be used during the study group
- Additional material provided as needed

Agenda:

9:00	**Introduction of session**
9:30	**Jigsaw—Read Article 1, 2, or 3**
	Identify underlying assumptions, key elements, and implementation requirements
9:55	**Discuss the reading**
	Structure—Think-Pair-Share
	Think: reflect on reading
	Pair: share in pairs ideas from reading
	Share: using a Round Robin—share with whole team
10:30	**Issues—discussion of the following questions with your team:**
	1. In what situations would you use study groups?
	2. What can I do to facilitate the use of study groups in schools with which I work?
	3. How do I customize study groups for these schools?

4. How can we use the study groups to learn more about the National Science Education Standards?

11:15   **Share discussion issues**

Structure—One-Astray

Number off in your teams

Number 2s in each team move right to the next team and share their home teams' answers to the issues questions. This is done two times and the one astray returns to his/her home team to share information from the two teams that were visited.

11:30   **Final discussion question:**

Based on the reading and discussions, with particular attention paid to the commentary at the end of the section, how can we facilitate a school's implementation of the study group strategy in its professional development plan so that:

1. the strategy is sustainable over time, and

2. it becomes integrated into the school's culture?

Structure—Round Robin with a recorder

Each member of the team shares one idea at a time, the #4 member records the ideas

Structure—Stand up & Share

Each team designates a "sharer"a and that person stands and shares the recorded ideas from a Round Robin. Each sharer from each team will share one item from his/her list. No ideas will be repeated, members from each team will check off same/similar ideas as they are heard. The sharer from each team will remain standing until all the ideas from that team's list are heard. Once all the ideas from your team's list are shared, your sharer sits down. After everyone is seated, the facilitator will know that all the ideas from all teams have been shared.

12:00   **Close and Evaluation**

SAMPLE 3: "At a Glance" Agenda for Multiday Conference

Comprehensive Professional Development Institute
July 27-31—Merrimack, NH
Institute Schedule

Time	Sunday, 7/27	Monday, 7/28	Tuesday, 7/29	Wednesday, 7/30	Thursday, 7/31
7:00 a.m.		Facilitator Breakfast 7-8 a.m.	Breakfast 7-8 a.m.	Breakfast 7-8 a.m.	Breakfast 7-8 a.m.
8:00		Participant Registration 8-10	Presentations Strand 1 (6 concurrent) 8 - 9:15	Presentations Strand 3 (6 concurrent) 8 - 9:15	Team Preparation 8 - 8:30
9:00			Presentations Strand 2 (6 concurrent) 9:30 - 10:45	Presentation Strand 4 (6 concurrent) 9:30 - 10:45	Critical Friends 8:30 - 11:00 (or TEAM TIME)
10:00	Facilitator Registration 10-12N	General Session 10 - 11			
11:00		Team Time 11 - 12N	Team Time 11 - 12N	Team Time 11-12N	Team Time 11-12N
12 Noon	LUNCH	LUNCH	LUNCH	LUNCH	Lunch and Closing Comments
1:00 p.m. 2:00 3:00 4:00	Facilitator Orientation #3 1 - 5	Team Time 1 - 4:15	Team Time 1 - 4:15	Team Time 1 - 4:15	Presentation of Products "Show Case" 1 - 2:30 or TEAM TIME
5:00	Tour & Team Rm Check	Facilitator Debrief 4:30 - 5:30	Facilitator Debrief 4:30 - 5:30	Facilitator Debrief 4:30 - 5:30	Facilitator DEBRIEF 3 - 4 pm
6:00 7:00	Dinner 6-7	Dinner 6-7	Dinner On Own	BBQ - Celebration	
8:00 9:00 10:00 p.m.		Making Change Game 7 - 10 p.m.	Informal Chat: Is There a Public for Public Education: A Community Dialogue 7:30-9:00 and/or Game Night	Team Skits	

73

SAMPLE 4: Schedule for a One-Day Conference

Event Number	Time	Activity	Location
1	8:30 A.M.	Registration	Lobby
2	9:00 A.M.	General session	Grand Ballroom
3	9:30 A.M.	Concurrent sessions	See Schedule
4	10:30 A.M.	Break	Lobby
5	10:45 A.M.	Concurrent sessions	See Schedule
6	11:30 A.M.	Free/Networking	
7	12:00 Noon	Lunch	North Salon
8	1:30 P.M.	Workshops I	See Schedule
9	2:30 P.M.	Concurrent sessions	See Schedule
10	3:15 P.M.	Break	
11	3:30 P.M.	Workshops II/ Evaluation	See Schedule

SAMPLE 5: Work Session Agenda

Day One
6:30 Dinner

Welcome and Overview

Refining and launching our work

Agenda review/purpose

Introduction

Getting to know each other and our organizations

Building the Foundation

As you reflect on your previous experience designing leadership development institutes or initiatives, what are the key lessons you've learned?

Day Two
8:00   **Continental Breakfast**

Informal revisiting of "Building the Foundation" discussion

8:30   **Begin Morning Discussions**

Project Overview and Discussion

Overview of the proposed design

Feedback on the guiding principles, expectations, and proposed design

Discuss needs assessment

Discuss the roles of the collaborating organizations

Develop Recruitment Strategies

Identify qualifications and expectations for participation

How do we serve the least served?

Discuss proposed idea of reserving "slots" for individuals

How do we best allocate our resources?

Design recruitment and application process

12:30   **Afternoon Discussion**

Designing for Content

How is this Academy specific to science and mathematics?

Evaluation Design

How will we know we have succeeded?

Review proposed evaluation design

Sharing Resources

Identify materials/resources for Fellows and Mentors

Wrap Up and Next Steps

Plan next meeting

Design recruitment brochure

4:00   **Evaluation/Close**

Resource C

Sample Evaluations

SAMPLE 1: Evaluation of Third Annual NISE Forum

February 23-24, 1998

The views of every participant are valued and will help us improve the NISE efforts on behalf of Science, Mathematics, Engineering and Technology Education.

(Circle the number that most closely matches your opinion)

	none	a little	some-what	a lot	a great deal
1. How much did you GAIN from the following plenary sessions?					
a. Panel 1: Evaluating Teaching, Learning, and Curriculum Changes in SMET Classrooms *Spencer, Ebert-May, Mazur, D. Porter, Fortenberry*	*(1)*	*(2)*	*(3)*	*(4)*	*(5)*

Comments:

b. Panel 2: Assessing Learning as an
Aspect of Change in Classrooms,
Disciplines,
and Institutions
Seymour, Coppola, Lewis, Tapia, *(1)*   *(2)*   *(3)*   *(4)*   *(5)*
Chubin
Comments:

c. Panel 3: Exploring the Role of
Evaluation in Changes at the
Departmental, Institutional, and
National Levels
Adelman, Bristol, Gomez,   *(1)*   *(2)*   *(3)*   *(4)*   *(5)*
Sheppard, Suter
Comments:

2. How much did you GAIN from these activities:
a. Reading the panelists' papers   *(1)*   *(2)*   *(3)*   *(4)*   *(5)*
b. Attending small discussions   *(1)*   *(2)*   *(3)*   *(4)*   *(5)*
c. Writing the think pieces   *(1)*   *(2)*   *(3)*   *(4)*   *(5)*
d. Participating in the poster session *(1)*   *(2)*   *(3)*   *(4)*   *(5)*
e. Other opportunities for networking *(1)*   *(2)*   *(3)*   *(4)*   *(5)*
Comments:

3. How much did you GAIN from the   *(1)*   *(2)*   *(3)*   *(4)*   *(5)*
forum OVERALL?

4. What do you plan to do with what
you gained from the forum?

5. Other comments:

THANK YOU VERY MUCH FOR YOUR TIME AND ATTENTION!

PLEASE RETURN THIS SURVEY BEFORE LEAVING THE FORUM.

Staff is on hand to collect forms as you leave the final session. In addition, "Survey Return" boxes are available at the registration table.

P.S. If you left the Forum without returning this form, please send it by March 3 to:
NISE Formative Evaluation
LEAD Center
1402 University Avenue, Room 413
University of Wisconsin-Madison
Madison, WI 53706

SAMPLE 2: Participant Evaluation: Professional Development Institute

Background Information

Please provide the following information for evaluation purposes only. Data will be presented in aggregate form only. (Your responses will remain confidential.)

1. Please put a check mark next to your role as a participant in this Institute:

    Teacher   (___elementary, ___middle, ___high school)
    Career/Guidance Counselor   (___elementary, ___middle, ___high school)
    School Building Administrator (___elementary, ___middle, ___high school)
    School District Administrator (please specify position) _____
    Other School District Staff (please specify position) _____
    School Board Member ___ Parent Team Member ___ Community Member ___
    Higher Education Faculty or Staff ___ Business Partner/Leader ___
    Other (please specify position) _____

2. (OPTIONAL) Please tell us the name of your team. _____

Institute Facilities
Please rate the following on the scale provided from *Excellent* to *Very Poor:*

1. Meeting rooms	Excellent	Good	Fair	Poor	Very Poor
2. Sleeping accommodations	Excellent	Good	Fair	Poor	Very Poor
3. Food	Excellent	Good	Fair	Poor	Very Poor

Comments:

Pre-Institute Session
Please indicate how valuable you, as a team member, found the pre-Institute session in terms of the following:

A. Identifying a significant task to be addressed during the Institute
    (Extremely valuable)   *(5)*   *(4)*   *(3)*   *(2)*   *(1)*   *(Not valuable at all)*

B. Understanding the Authentic Task Approach to be used during the Institute
    (Extremely valuable)   *(5)*   *(4)*   *(3)*   *(2)*   *(1)*   *(Not valuable at all)*

C. Deciding how to make the best use of resource people during the Institute
    (Extremely valuable)   *(5)*   *(4)*   *(3)*   *(2)*   *(1)*   *(Not valuable at all)*

D. Establishing an appropriate mix of team participants for optimal planning and decision making
    (Extremely valuable)   *(5)*   *(4)*   *(3)*   *(2)*   *(1)*   *(Not valuable at all)*

Comments:

Your Team's Authentic Task

1. Please very briefly describe the task your team chose to address during the Institute.

2. How, if at all, do you believe that your plan/project/task will have an impact on what students in your school, district, or region will know and be able to do?

3. What has your team done to ensure that your plan/project/task is systemic in approach?

4. To what extent do you believe that your team successfully accomplished its task during the Institute?

   (To a great extent)   *(5)*   *(4)*   *(3)*   *(2)*   *(1)*   *(Not at all)*

5. To what extent did your team's facilitators contribute to the accomplishment of your task?

   (To a great extent)   *(5)*   *(4)*   *(3)*   *(2)*   *(1)*   *(Not at all)*

6. Please indicate and briefly explain which other Institute resources (people, printed resources, presentations) were most useful to your team in accomplishing your task. Please be specific in telling us how you used these resources.

7. Please indicate and briefly explain any serious frustrations you experienced while working on your team's task.

8. What next steps has your team identified for your plan/project/task?

9. To what extent do you understand your own role in following through on your plan/project/task?

   (To a great extent)   *(5)*   *(4)*   *(3)*   *(2)*   *(1)*   *(Not at all)*

10. What concerns do you have (or what obstacles do you anticipate), if any, about carrying through with your plan/project/task over the next year?

    What strategies, if any, have you already identified to address these?

11. What plans have you made, if any, to continue working with your facilitator(s) in the future?

Effectiveness of Institute Components

1. Please rate each of the following components of the Institute in terms of its value to you and your team in accomplishing your tasks and in learning effective ways of working together. Please briefly explain each of your responses.

   a. Outside facilitation of your team's work

   (Extremely valuable)   *(5)*   *(4)*   *(3)*   *(2)*   *(1)*   *(Not valuable at all)*

   Please Explain.

   b. Time to work together on your task

   (Extremely valuable)   *(5)*   *(4)*   *(3)*   *(2)*   *(1)*   *(Not valuable at all)*

   Please Explain.

   c. Development and use of rubrics

   (Extremely valuable)   *(5)*   *(4)*   *(3)*   *(2)*   *(1)*   *(Not valuable at all)*

   Please Explain.

   d. Development and use of team portfolio

   (Extremely valuable)   *(5)*   *(4)*   *(3)*   *(2)*   *(1)*   *(Not valuable at all)*

   Please Explain.

   e. Information-intnesive workshops.

   (Extremely valuable)   *(5)*   *(4)*   *(3)*   *(2)*   *(1)*   *(Not valuable at all)*

   Please Explain.

   f. Opportunity to meet with presenters/resource colleagues

   (Extremely valuable)   *(5)*   *(4)*   *(3)*   *(2)*   *(1)*   *(Not valuable at all)*

   Please Explain.

   g. Time to reflect on learning

   (Extremely valuable)   *(5)*   *(4)*   *(3)*   *(2)*   *(1)*   *(Not valuable at all)*

   Please Explain.

   h. Help/troubleshooting from Institute staff

   (Extremely valuable)   *(5)*   *(4)*   *(3)*   *(2)*   *(1)*   *(Not valuable at all)*

   Please Explain.

2.   Please share with us what you believe was the greatest strength of this Institute.

3.   Please indicate any suggestions you have for how this Institute could have been more effective.

Follow-Up to This Institute

Please indicate if you would be interested in participating in activities throughout the coming year as a follow-up to this Institute?

                    Yes   *No*   *Uncertain*

If YES, please give suggestions for the format and topical focus that would be most useful to you.

FORMAT:

TOPICAL FOCUS:

THANK YOU FOR COMPLETING THIS EVALUATION! Please return the form to the EVALUATIONS box at the Registration Desk before leaving the Institute.

SOURCE: Sample 2 of Resource C is adapted with permission from Learning Innovations (1997), a division of WestEd.

References

Bolman, L. G., & Deal, T. E. (1992). *Reframing organizations: Artistry, choice, and leadership.* San Francisco, CA: Jossey-Bass.

Brooks, J. G., & Brooks, M. G. (1993). *In search of understanding: The case for constructivist classrooms.* Alexandria, VA: Association for Supervision and Curriculum Development.

Bybee, R. (1997). *Achieving scientific literacy: From purposes to practices.* Portsmouth, NH: Heinemann.

Donohue, N., Dunne, K., & Phlegar, J. (1999). *The authentic task approach: A powerful strategy to promote professional learning and change.* Stoneham, MA: Learning Innovations.

Friel, S. N., & Bright, G. W. (Eds.). (1997). *Reflecting on our work: NSF teacher enhancement in K-6 mathematics.* Lanham, MD: University Press of America.

Garmston, R., & Wellman, B. (1998). *The adaptive school developing and facilitating collaborative groups.* El Dorado Hills, CA: Four Hats Seminars.

Garmston, R. J., & Wellman, B. M. (1992). *How to make presentations that teach and transform.* Alexandria, VA: Association for Supervision and Curriculum Development.

Hutchinson, J., & Huberman, M. (1993). *Knowledge dissemination and use in science and mathematics education: A literature review.* Washington, DC: The National Science Foundation.

Learning Innovations. (1997). *The New Hampshire professional development institute.* Stoneham, MA: Author.

Loucks-Horsley, S., Harding, C. K., Arbuckle, M. A., Murray, L. B., Dubea, C., & Williams, M. K. (1987). *Continuing to learn: A guidebook for teacher development.* Stoneham, MA: Learning Innovations.

Loucks-Horsley, S., Hewson, P. W., Love, N., & Stiles, K. E. (1998). *Designing professional development for teachers of science and mathematics.* Thousand Oaks, CA: Corwin.

Mason, S., Gunter, R., Miller, S. & Seymour, E. (1998). Synthesis of think piece essays: Voices from the field. In S. Millar (Ed.), *Synthesis and proceedings of the third annual NISE forums.* Madison, WI: National Institute for Science Education.

Mundry, S. E., & Loucks-Horsley, S. (1999). *Designing decision points and dilemmas* (NISE Brief, Vol. 3, No. 1). Madison, WI: National Institute for Science Education.

Nadler, L., & Nadler, Z. (1987). *The comprehensive guide to successful conferences and meetings.* San Francisco, CA: Jossey-Bass.

Polivka, E. G. (Ed.). (1996). *Professional meeting management* (3rd ed.). Birmingham, AL: Professional Convention Management Association.

Ramsborg, G. C. (1995). *Objectives to outcomes: Your contract with the learner* (2nd ed.). Birmingham, AL: Professional Convention Management Association.

Scholtes, P. R., Joiner, B., & Streibel, B. J. (1996). *The team handbook* (2nd ed.). Madison, WI: Joiner Associates.

Senge, P. M. (1990). *The fifth discipline: The art and practice of the learning organization.* NY: Doubleday.

Senge, P. M., Keiner, A., Roberts, C., Ross, R. & Smith, B. (1994). *The fifth discipline fieldbook: Strategies and tools for building a learning organization.* New York: Doubleday.

Sparks, D., & Hirsch, S. (1997). *A new vision for staff development.* Oxford, OH: National Staff Development Council.

Sprinthall, N. A., & Sprinthall, L. T. (1983). The teacher as adult learner: A cognitive-development view. In *Staff Development:* The yearbook of the National Society for the Study of Education. Chicago: University of Chicago Press.

Thompson, C. L., & Zeuli, J. S. (2000). The frame and the tapestry: Standards-based reform and professional development. In G. Sykes (Ed.), *The heart of the matter: Teaching as the learning profession.* San Francisco: Jossey-Bass.

Vaill, P. B. (1996). *Learning as a way of being.* San Francisco, CA: Jossey-Bass.

Index